The Lutterworth Press
P.O. Box 60
Cambridge
CB1 2NT
United Kingdom

www.lutterworth.com
publishing@lutterworth.com

Paperback ISBN: 978 0 7188 9513 6
PDF ISBN: 978 0 7188 4793 7
ePub ISBN: 978 0 7188 4794 4
Kindle ISBN: 978 0 7188 4795 1

British Library Cataloguing in Publication Data
A record is available from the British Library

First published by The Lutterworth Press, 2019

FIGURE 1 (previous page):
Close-up of Diana's faithful hunting hounds
- Lviv, Ukraine (See Chapter 1).

FIGURE 2 (Contents verso):
Seaman, a well-travelled dog who helped map and
investigate the western United States (Sioux City
Interpretive Center, USA) (see Chapter 7).

To mum and dad,
for their pet loving genes and much more...

In support of BLUE CROSS FOR PETS
Pets change lives
We change theirs

Our gratitude to our crowdfunding contributors:

Janet Hoptroff
The Goldsmith family: Bea, Ruth, Tom and the cat Zozo
Jill Cobb
Doug Hey
Jane Patrick
Caroline Evans
Mrs Doreen Yeates
Martin Barnes
Jean Summers
John Witton

Monumental Tales

The fascinating stories behind the world's pet statues and memorials

Jackie Buckle

foreword by
Chris Packham

The Lutterworth Press

Contents

FIGURE 3: Chris Packham with his much-loved pet Poodle, Scratchy.

FIGURE 4: Old Shep, one of America's many monuments to a faithful canine companion
(Fort Benton, MT) (See Chapter 2).

Foreword

Gravestones leave me with mixed feelings. Some, such as the First World War graves, pertinently mark significant moments in our history. I once toured those fields of white stones in France and, although I had no known relatives laid to rest there, I was profoundly moved by their horrific scale and overwhelmed by an enormous sense of tragedy. Curiously, it was the impersonality that was so affecting: 'Known Unto God' over and over and over again. These tombstones carry a large, powerful, and important message to us all over many years.

But the overblown and vainglorious statuary marking the graves of the long-gone idle rich leave me dead cold. How dare they think that we would continue to care? The cheek of it! I'm so pleased to see their aspirations of immortality neglected and overgrown by nature and to know their bodily remains have fed the ivy that obscures their names. Most graves are aptly temporary in the grand scheme of things, tended for two or three generations at most while they play a critical part in the painful grieving process. After that, their job is done. Few of us are important enough to be remembered for any longer.

The memorials catalogued here are different. Of course, for the owners or carers of the dogs and cats they are a place to contemplate their loss, but collectively they say a lot about us. This fascinating and revealing book spans the globe and a vast range of ages, but I challenge you to read any one account and not feel empathy for the animal they celebrate. It leaps from heartbreak to wonder, from heroism to love, and from joy back to heartbreak again. And the tales in themselves are remarkable, surprising, and entertaining. Some of the animals are familiar, but others not so much. Most dog lovers will have heard of Greyfriars Bobby, but few will know the truth behind this amazing story. Some tell tales of fame from overseas: Balto the sled dog, once a national treasure in the United States, and Tombili the portly cat from Istanbul that caused an Internet sensation. And the book even rewrites history. Ernest Shackleton has always been a hero of mine – his boat journey across the south polar seas to rescue his men was hugely inspirational. It was made possible through the skills of the carpenter who had adapted their vessel to withstand the harsh environs. But now I've learned that 'The Boss' (Shackleton) had the carpenter's cat shot and that the carpenter was denied the coveted Polar Medal. Maybe Sir E was not the man I thought he was!

I honestly couldn't put this book down, perhaps because collectively these stories are a fitting memorial and reassuring reminder that, for all our human ills, our deep love for our companion animals is truly immortal.

Chris Packham
New Forest, 2018

Introduction and thanks

Wandering along a quiet London street on a hot August afternoon while flicking through my A-Z map book, I walked right into a cat on the pavement. Luckily, the cat didn't mind too much since he was enclosed by iron railings and made of stone.

Being someone who has a fondness for animals (cats and dogs in particular), I took a closer look and saw that the railings displayed a plaque with a mobile phone code. Curious, I swiped my phone and was taken aback when the statue came to life with the voice of Helen Lederer. I placed my ear closer to the speaker and tried to listen, though it was difficult with the many buses that chose that moment to roar past.

'Am I male or am I female?' purred the cat (or more accurately, Helen). 'Am I myth or am I truth?'

Then I noticed another plaque that revealed this to be none other than Dick Whittington's cat, marking the very spot where Dick reputedly heard the Bow Bells tell him to 'Turn again, Dick Whittington, thrice Lord Mayor of London.' It was all quite surprising and rather wonderful.

Back home, later that day, I began to investigate the statue some more. As the Internet is wont to do, I found myself taken off to hundreds of related statue stories. I discovered the tales behind many of these to be touching, intriguing, sometimes funny, and, it must be said, occasionally pretty weird.

In short, this chance encounter with a limestone moggie led to my becoming a little obsessed by these pets who have been immortalised as monuments. I have loved bringing some of the more interesting of these tales together here and I hope you enjoy reading them.

A Big Thank You

Around a third of the photographs in this book came from people on Flickr (the photo-sharing website) who gladly let me use their wonderful shots and without whom the book would not exist. They are credited at the end. Please do check them out; they have done some excellent work.

I would also like to thank Helen Cobb for taking some beautiful pictures for me. Plus Ian King and Jean-Pierre Collin for their superb shots of Gelert's grave and Le Cimetiere Des Animaux Domestiques.

I spoke to and met with some incredibly interesting people while working on this project. Thanks so much to Katherine Barnett from Chartwell for introducing me to Jock the Cat, to Clive who showed me round Hyde Park Pet Cemetery, and to PC Paul Nicholls who filled me with enthusiasm for his national memorial to UK police dogs.

Thanks to Alison Hobson of Fairford History Society, Rita James of CAGED, and Patrick Roberts who runs the brilliant Purr 'n' Fur website. I am

FIGURE 5: Dick Whittington's cat.

also indebted to Dr Eric Tourigny who shared some fascinating information about pet cemeteries, and to Joel Walker who created the Ruswarp statue and was happy to provide interesting insights into her work.

Some of my enquiries took me overseas, at least by email! Thanks to Yuta Sakaguchi for his *Maneki* cat information, Travis Souther at the Abraham Lincoln Museum, Anadolu Kedisi in Istanbul, and the Russian cat blogger Bz Viola.

I suspect that many people may be tempted to pick up this book because it mentions their wildlife hero Chris Packham on the cover. Thanks so much to Chris for helping with this venture and writing the book's foreword. I am also indebted to my good friend John Witton who proofread the manuscript.

Finally, thank you to my daughters, Sophie and Jasmine, for all their help and input. And of course a big hug for my dog, Lexi, whose picture I have managed to shoehorn into the text here and there and who is one of the reasons I can get up each morning with a smile on my face.

DISCLAIMER

Why no horses? you may well ask. My apologies that we decided not to include horse statues. There are such a large number of them – many military in nature – that they really deserve a book of their own.

I should also clarify that I am merely a pet and history enthusiast and not a qualified historian. For a more in-depth and scholarly coverage of many of these topics, Hilda Kean has an informative website – hildakean.com

Finally, while I have included a selection of places where you can see various monuments, this is by no means exhaustive. After completing the first draft of this book I became aware of a new project being run by Eric Tourigny at Newcastle University. Eric is hoping to create a database of pet memorials and is encouraging people to use the Ancient Animals app from Exeter University to report any they discover. You can find out more by searching for Finding Fido on the Newcastle University website. And please do contact me too with any discoveries, observations, pictures, etc. I'd love to hear from you.

monumentaltales.org.uk

FIGURE 6: Pet animals are an endless source of companionship and fun.

FIGURE 7: Mother of all cats? The beautiful African wildcat – *Felis sylvestris lybica*.

CHAPTER I

A potted history of pets

AS REVEALED THROUGH THEIR STATUES

WITH OUR LOVE OF technology and our busy need to be in several places at once, we have little time these days to register monuments like the impressive winged horse in the city square, let alone the little dog statue in the neglected park. But if you can take time to notice these things, you will often be rewarded with a fascinating story of the attachment between ourselves and animals.

As a pet bereavement support worker for the Blue Cross, I have often witnessed the incredible bond between people and their pets. Reasons for this vary of course, but some of the main theories relate to our need for emotional support, our desire to be caregivers, and our wish to relate to another species. There is also some evidence emerging for a genetic component to the desire to have pets.[1] (So the next time you are mopping up pet wee from the carpet you can blame your parents!)

While the evidence for a beneficial effect from pet ownership is not unequivocal, many owners can point to ways in which animals enhance their lives, such as, for example, assisting them in keeping active. Perhaps most of all, people often find that pets provide dependable, non-judgemental companionship that helps them to live in the moment and forget the problems of the past or the worries of the future.

So when did this amazing relationship start?

THE FIRST PET DOGS

There's a fair amount of debate over when animals became domesticated, but what is largely agreed upon is that dogs were first and they probably evolved from the Eurasian grey wolf. Genetic research suggests this may have happened around 30,000 years ago. Scientists think that the process of domestication probably began during the last Ice Age in South East Asia.[2] Conditions were harsh and wolves would have begun scavenging in campsites for food, gradually growing less and less timid around us.

Over time, animals evolved through selective breeding to show more of the desirable characteristics we value in dogs today – loyalty, a good temperament, and biddability. These early dogs would have helped their Stone Age masters with hunting, guarding, and herding.

However, archaeological evidence suggests that such dogs could be much more than working animals to their owners. One of the earliest such finds is from Israel and reveals a 14,000-year-old human buried with his arm positioned around a puppy in a way that suggests a strong affection.[3] In Germany, another Stone Age discovery shows a man and woman buried together with their dog. The poor animal looks to have suffered various illnesses that would have probably proven fatal without the intensive care of its owners.

Excavations of burial grounds in Siberia from around 5,000-8,000 years ago also reveal graves with dogs buried beside their humans. Some of the animals wore highly decorative collars and were found lying beside items such as spoons and bowls, which may have been for them to take to the afterlife.[4] It seems, then, that we have long cherished our canine companions.

FIGURE 8: Gayer-Anderson cat statue – a representation of the cat deity Bastet.

FIGURE 9 (opposite): Recumbent statue of Anubis recovered from the tomb of Tutankhamun.

THE FIRST PET CATS

As with dogs, it hasn't been easy for historians to work out when cats were domesticated. In 2004, a Neolithic grave on the island of Cyprus was found to contain the skeletons of a human and cat laid close together.[5] This burial site is estimated to be around 9,500 years old. The cat skeleton is larger than our present-day moggies, which ties in with genetic research suggesting today's cats probably descend from the African and Near Eastern Wildcat, *Felis sylvestris lybica*.

The authors of this research believe that cats may well have been domesticated in the Middle East, in an area known as the Fertile Crescent. It was here, around 12,000 years ago, that agriculture first developed.

This association of cat domestication with humans settling down, growing and storing crops makes perfect sense because with grain stores came the cat's favourite prey – mice. The first cats to arrive on the scene must have felt like they'd reached kitty heaven and the farmers would have no doubt been pleased to be rid of all their grain-eating pests.

ANCIENT WORLDS
Egypt

Although dogs and cats were kept by the ancient Egyptians, it is cats that we tend to associate most with this period, largely because the Egyptians were rather obsessed with them. Drawings and statues of the Egyptian goddess Bastet, depicted as a cat or woman with a cat's head, are widespread throughout Egyptian archaeology. As well as being the goddess of cats, Bastet was also associated with pregnancy, motherhood, and protection against evil.

The Egyptians ascribed many powers to their felines. They were impressed by the animal's ability to see in the dark and believed they controlled the moon's movement. Many temples had resident cats that were greatly fussed over by priests. And anyone found guilty of killing a cat was sentenced to death! It was also strictly prohibited to export them. In fact, there was even a branch of government dedicated to finding exported cats and bringing them back to Egypt.

According to the Greek historian Herodotus, who visited Egypt around 450 BC, when a pet cat died the whole family would go into mourning and engage in rituals that, somewhat surprisingly, included shaving their eyebrows.[6] And if a house caught fire it was imperative that the cats inside were rescued, regardless of the risk to human life. I'm not sure how reliable a commentator Herodotus was though, as he also describes how people had to create a human barrier to prevent their cats from leaping back into the flames! That does seem a tad unlikely.

What is certain is that after death, pet cats were mummified and buried in a temple dedicated to Bastet. Extraordinary numbers of these cat mummies were excavated at the end of the nineteenth century and brought to the UK; so many, in fact, that it was suggested they be crushed up and used as fertiliser or ballast for ships.

'In our ever-changing culture animals have remained constant and, whilst soothing as well as invigorating our lives, they have given us cheerful support through the ages.'

Lucinda Lambton

'In ancient times, cats were worshipped as gods. They have not forgotten this.'

Terry Pratchett

The cult of Bastet lasted for over 2,000 years before it was banned by the Romans in AD 390. The Egyptian legacy lives on though, through their many statues, paintings, and possibly even through their language. It seems likely that the words for cat used today in many European languages (*chat*/France, *kat*/Denmark, *katze*/German, *gatto*/Italy, *qattus*/Malta) may well derive from the original Egyptian word – *quattah*.

Despite this amazing reverence for cats, dogs were valued in Egypt too, and when they died they would also often be mummified and buried with great ceremony and more brow shaving. The Egyptian's belief in the afterlife meant that dogs were often interred with their masters so they could remain companions after death. Sometimes pet dogs were placed in specially constructed coffins and buried in dog cemeteries. Archaeologists have found names inscribed upon these coffins such as 'Brave one', 'Reliable', 'Good Herdsman', and the slightly more prosaic 'Blacky', presumably referring to the animal's colour. One poor dog was even given the name 'Useless'.[7]

One of the most famous Egyptian gods was the dog-like Anpu, more commonly referred to by his Greek name, Anubis. Anubis was thought to be modelled on the Egyptian jackals who were seen wandering around burial sites. Recent genetic testing has revealed, however, that rather than being jackals, these animals were Africa's only member of the grey wolf family.[8]

Anubis was the god of mummification who oversaw burial rights and guided the passage of the deceased to the afterlife. He is represented as a man with a jackal head or as a black dog. Black is thought to have been chosen, as it signifies death yet is reminiscent of regeneration through its association with the fertile dark soils of the Nile. In tomb paintings and engravings, Anubis is often seen kneeling beside a pair of golden scales on which he weighs the Heart of the Soul against the Feather of Truth.

Greeks and Romans

Egyptian rulers were replaced by Greeks during the occupation of Egypt in the Ptolemaic Dynasty. However, it appears that the Greeks adopted and continued to worship many of the Egyptian animal deities, even if they interpreted them in their own way. In 2010, archaeologists were amazed to discover a Greek temple from the third century BC that was dedicated to the Egyptian goddess Bastet and filled with thousands of stone cat statues.[9]

Like the Egyptians, both the Greeks and Romans seemed enamoured by their companion animals. Many Greek and Roman graveyards dedicated to pets have been discovered and some of the tombs therein have particularly touching inscriptions:

My eyes were wet with tears, our little dog, when I bore thee (to the grave) . . .

So, Patricus, never again shall thou give me a thousand kisses. Never canst thou be contentedly in my lap. In sadness have I buried

FIGURE 10: Diana statue
(fountain on the Rynok square), Lviv, Ukraine.

FIGURE 11 (opposite): Dog of Alcibiades
at Petworth Park, West Sussex, UK.

thee, and thou deservist. In a resting place of
marble, I have put thee for all time by the side
of my shade. In thy qualities, sagacious thou
wert like a human being.

Ah, me! What a loved companion have we
lost![10]

One of the best-known Roman goddesses, and
one who is thought to have inspired many heroines
seen in today's comic books and computer games,
was Diana. This feisty young woman was goddess of
the hunt and domestic animals, and many sculptures
feature her beside her faithful hunting hounds.

According to Roman mythology, she and Orion
were due to be married, but Diana's brother, Apollo,
disapproved and tricked his sister into slaying
Orion in a shooting test. Diana was so distraught
at accidentally killing her lover that she made him
into a constellation in the sky along with his hunting
dogs, Canis Major and Canis Minor.

One of the few original Roman sculptures of pets
still in existence in the UK is the so-called 'Dog of
Alcibiades', or Jennings Dog. This statue is a marble
copy of a bronze Molossian hound from ancient
Greece. Molossian hounds are now extinct, but many
of today's larger breeds such as mastiffs, St Bernards,
and Great Danes are thought to be their descendants.
Historians believe these giant dogs were used for
hunting and, kitted out with protective armour and
spiked collars, fought with elephants, lions, and
tigers.[11]

The 'Dog of Alcibiades' was discovered in the 1750s
when the English collector Henry Jennings visited
an antiques shop in Rome and spied it beneath a
pile of rubble.[12] He bought it for around £80 – a
not inconsiderable sum – and brought it back with
him to Britain. The statue was intact, but the tail
had broken off, and this led Jennings to name it the
'Dog of Alcibiades' after an Athenian statesman who
is supposed to have confounded everyone by buying
a large dog with a beautiful tail that he then cut off![12]

Jennings is quoted as saying, 'I was offered £1,400
for my purchase but I would not part with my dog.
I had bought it for myself and liked to contemplate
his fine proportions and admire him at my leisure.'[12]

In 1778, Jennings reluctantly did have to sell his
beloved statue to pay off his gambling debts, so the
dog went to stay with Charles Duncombe MP in
Duncombe Park, Yorkshire. In 1925, Duncombe
Park was leased out as a girls' school. Here the pupils
apparently liked to wipe their dirty hands on their
much-loved dog to save washing them and would
also feed it their unwanted marmite sandwiches![13]

STATUES OF DIANA

You can see the beautiful Diana with her hounds in many locations: Powerscourt Demesne, Enniskerry, Co. Wicklow, Ireland; Wellington Parade and Clarendon Street, Melbourne, Australia; Fontainebleau, Seine-et-Marne, France; Musée du Louvre, Paris, France; and Rynok Square, Lviv, Ukraine.

THE DOG OF ALCIBIADES

See the stone Molossers in Victoria Park, Grove Road, London E3 5TB and at Petworth House, Park Road, Petworth GU28 0AE (National Trust). The marble Roman original is at the British Museum, Gallery 22, Great Russell Street, London.

In 2001, when the school was sold, it looked like the dog would be bought by an American museum. Thankfully, some desperate, last-minute fundraising enabled Britain to retain the statue and you can now see this wonderful, ancient dog in his forever home at the British Museum.

The popularity of the 'Dog of Alcibiades' design led to a large number of stone copies being sculpted. A pair still sits in Victoria Park in east London and there are others in various National Trust properties throughout England, including Petworth House where the Third Earl of Egremont had one created as a memorial to his favourite dog that drowned in the lake there.

Meanwhile in Asia

While cats and dogs began spreading throughout Europe during the Roman period, many thousands of miles away in Asia they were also making their presence felt. In ancient Chinese society the dog played important roles in hunting, as guards, and in mythology. The dog is one of twelve animals in the Chinese zodiac with people born under its sign said to possess the traits of loyalty, trustworthiness, and kindness. And yet, it seems the relationship was complicated since, according to early Chinese records, dogs were also used as a source of meat – a practice that sadly still occurs today.

Cats were worshipped widely in Asia, as shown by the Indian cat deity, Sastht, and the Chinese cat goddess, Li Shou. Perhaps the most famous of the Asian felines is the Japanese Beckoning or Fortune Cat (*Maneki neko*).

The exact origins of *Maneki neko* are unknown, but a painting from 1852 features a variation of the little cat being sold at the Sensō-ji temple, in Akasusa, Tokyo. Around the Imado Shrine in Akasusa, a great many *Maneki neko* statues were made, and the shrine and its surrounding precincts are still home to a fantastically large number.

There are lots of legends around *Maneki neko*, but one of the most popular goes as follows: a wealthy nobleman was sheltering beneath a tree when he saw a cat in a nearby poor temple summoning him with an upraised paw. The nobleman went over to the cat and just as he entered the temple, the tree he'd been standing under was struck by lightning. Understandably grateful after his narrow escape, the nobleman donated generously to the poor temple, and forever after this little cat has been associated with good luck and fortune.

Beckoning cats are now wildly popular with many being sold as gifts throughout the world. They are often found in shop windows where their upraised arms beckon people inside to spend their money. These little cats are even thought to be the inspiration behind the global phenomenon that is Hello Kitty. Perhaps the upraised paw was interpreted as waving hello in greeting?

Early Christianity

Christianity began to spread throughout the Roman Empire and into the Anglo-Saxon period. Cat and dog remains have been excavated from many Anglo-Saxon sites, so it seems likely these animals were familiar to our

Saxon ancestors. Early church adornments frequently featured animals and while these were often mythical in nature, dogs and cats did occasionally feature. The amazing gothic church of Westminster Abbey includes dogs on its flying buttresses, while the grinning 'Smithfield cat' can be spotted in London's oldest church – the beautiful St Bartholomew the Great. This decoration is actually a loadbearing stone or corbel. To me, it is very reminiscent of the Cheshire Cat in *Alice in Wonderland*. I wonder if Lewis Carroll ever saw it and was inspired. There are also the Templar cats of Temple Church, Fleet Street. All of these decorations date from around the twelfth century.

A number of early Christian saints are known for their association with domestic animals. St Roch, who is the patron saint of dogs, travelled around Italy ministering to the sick and was said to have performed many miraculous cures. After somewhat embarrassingly falling ill himself, however, he was expelled and forced to live in the forest. The story goes that he would have perished had not a dog belonging to a nobleman supplied him with bread and licked his wounds. Statues of St Roch often feature this canine saviour by his side.

It is St Francis, however, who is most commonly associated with animals. Born in Italy in 1181, St

Francis of Assisi cared for the poor and the sick and praised animals as brothers and sisters. In one famous story, St Francis tamed a wolf who was terrorising the Italian city of Gubbio. It is said that when the wolf ran at him, snarling and baring its fangs, he calmly made the sign of the cross and commanded the wolf to end its attacks. Next thing onlookers knew, the chastened animal was trotting up to St Francis, laying at his feet, and putting its head in his hands like a devoted dog.

This story is one of many in the Christian narrative that depict holy people being able to exert control over animals and nature. Statues of St Francis with animals are widespread and he remains one of the most popular saints. Every year on 4 October, Christians celebrate the Feast of St Francis by bringing their pets into church. Animals of all kinds, including rabbits, tortoises, and even spiders are blessed in churches on this day.

THE MIDDLE AGES AND TUDOR PERIOD

During the Middle Ages and Tudor period (13th-16th century), dogs became increasingly common throughout Europe for their use as hunting hounds. Hunting was a favourite pastime of the elite and was associated with wealth, status, and power.

Lapdogs were also starting to become popular and paintings, such as one of Queen Mary I and Prince

THE ANIMAL SAINTS
St Roch and his dog can be found in many locations. In the UK they can be seen at Salisbury Cathedral, 6 The Close, Salisbury SP1 2EJ. In France at the Church of Saint Roch, 296 Rue Saint Honoré, 75001 Paris, and Saint Augustin Church, 8 Avenue César Caire, 75008 Paris.
Statues of St Francis accompanied by animals may be found throughout the world. A lovely one in Sorrento, Italy, seemed to be a place to which many local 'stray' cats gravitated when I visited the town in 2005.

FIGURE 12 (opposite, left): Maneki Neko at Imado Shrine, Taito 111-0024, Tokyo Prefecture, Japan.

FIGURE 13 (opposite, right): St Roch and his devoted dog. West Front of Salisbury Cathedral.

FIGURE 14: Friendly-looking dog gargoyle at St Margaret's Church.

Philip from 1552,[14] show that toy spaniels often featured as pets in the Tudor period. The word 'pet' is recorded as early as 1530 with the meaning 'animal kept as a favourite', and it is probably associated with the word 'petty', from the French *petit*. It is thought that in addition to companionship they helped keep the Court ladies' laps warm in what were probably rather draughty surroundings.

King Charles II, who reigned from 1660-85, was also fond of spaniels and several varieties are seen in his portraits and now bear his name.

Despite this royal favour, the rise of the Christian Church was not particularly good news for domestic animals. The Church mainly disapproved of keeping pets, probably because of the association of animals with pagan symbolism and the Christian view that humans held dominion over nature's beasts.

During the witch trials of the sixteenth and seventeenth centuries, cats were particularly demonised. People with cats could be accused of being witches and put to death along with their pets (or 'familiars' as they were called). Rather heartbreakingly, it is thought that those living alone, who were perhaps elderly or socially isolated and kept pets for some much-needed company, were some of the most targeted.

It has been argued that this widespread destruction of cats may have led to an explosion in the numbers of rats and mice, and hence the numbers of fleas that have been implicated in transmitting the Black Death in the mid-fourteenth century.

In view of this antipathy towards cats, it is perhaps not surprising that they do not feature widely in paintings or sculptures of the period. For this reason a statue of the great statesman Cardinal Wolsey in his birth town of Ipswich is as unusual as it is endearing. It seems that the cardinal was a great lover of cats – a cat would sit with him during mass and was often at his side in formal meetings. It is said that Wolsey often took a couple along with him when meeting King Henry VIII. Perhaps they took the pressure off some of the more difficult conversations.

Thankfully, with the age of Enlightenment, science and logic began to impact upon people's lives more and more. Superstitious beliefs, such as in witchcraft, began to fade and cats (and their owners) could live freely again.

THE GEORGIANS AND VICTORIANS
During the 1700s and 1800s, the rise of the middle classes, combined with the well-known fondness of Queen Victoria for animals (see Chapter 3), meant

that pet-keeping for companionship boomed. This generated a whole new industry devoted to pet-related merchandise; the first dog food, for example, came to market in 1860. The Society for the Prevention of Cruelty to Animals was founded in 1824 and an increased awareness of the plight of animals was common throughout the Victorian period.

Throughout this period, the number of dog breeds grew greatly thanks to the efforts of people mating together dogs that possessed desirable characteristics (see Chapter 4). Today, there are 211 distinct dog breeds as recognised by the Kennel Club of the United Kingdom.[15] While this is more than were available in the 1800s, there were still many types for the Victorians to choose from and the new categorisation of breeds chimed with their love of order. In 1859, Newcastle was host to one of the world's first competitive dog shows, and the Kennel Club, which drew up a register of purebred dogs and their breed characteristics, came into being shortly after in 1873.

As we know, cat breeds show much less variety than dogs, no doubt because being independent in nature, cats have allowed us less control over who they breed with. There have also traditionally been fewer practical uses for cats, producing less demand for certain physical traits. However, the Victorians did selectively breed for coat colour and type, and

the first 'official' cat show was held at Crystal Palace in London on 13 July 1871.[16] This started a real craze for cat shows amongst the upper classes, both here and in the US.

Cats and Cigarettes

The popularity of cats may also have been buoyed up by a renewed interest in all things Egyptian brought on by the excavation of Tutankhamun's tomb in 1922.

Inspired by this ancient discovery, Don José Carreras Ferrer, the founder of the Carreras Cigarette Factory, had a pair of 8ft bronze cats installed at the entrance to his firm's offices on Hampstead Road in Camden.

This beautiful art deco building, constructed in 1928, was designed as a temple to Bastet, and the architects' plans suggest that it was originally to be called Bast House. The idea was dropped, however, as it sounded a little too much like Bastard House.

Carreras had long been a fan of cats and there was often a black one sleeping in the window of his little tobacconist shop on Wardour Street. The cat was such a regular fixture that the shop was soon referred to simply as the 'black cat shop'. Not surprising, then, that Don José chose the moggie to represent his company's branding and trademark. Carreras went on to produce the aptly named Black

CARDINAL WOLSEY
You can see Cardinal Wolsey and his cat at 1 St Peter's Street, Ipswich IP1 1XF.

THE CARRERAS CATS
See the Carreras cats at Greater London House, 180 Hampstead Road, London NW1 7AW. Use Mornington Crescent tube station.

THE LITTLE BROWN DOG
This statue brimming with history can be found in The English Garden, Battersea Park, London SW11 4NJ.

FIGURE 15 (opposite): Smiling cat in St Bartholomew the Great Church, London.

FIGURE 16: Wolsey, with his cat peeping out from behind his flowing robes, bottom left, Ipswich.

Cat cigarettes, which the firm sent to British soldiers in France during WWI. The packets even contained little French phrasebooks to help the Tommies make friends with their French allies.[17]

The Carreras cats currently at Greater London House are replicas that were added in 1996. Architects consulted the original plans for the building and restored it to its former glory after many of the wonderful art deco features had been removed or covered up in the 1960s. The building now houses a number of companies' offices. I wonder if many of the current staff are cat fans.

A LITTLE DOG AND A LOT OF TROUBLE
As Carreras was building his tobacco empire, a dog statue in south London was causing all sorts of problems, affording us an intriguing insight into the political activism of the time.

It started in 1903 when Professor Bayliss demonstrated an experiment on a small brown terrier in the University College of London's Department of Physiology during a lecture to medical students. Unbeknownst to him, two Swedish feminists had infiltrated the demonstration with a view to recording what went on. The ladies were very distressed to note that the dog was wounded from a previous experiment and was struggling, showing that it had not been properly anaesthetised. The

ladies were also dismayed that the lecture had been performed in a disrespectful atmosphere with the audience laughing.

Vivisection was a contentious issue then, as it is today, and it was against the law for an animal to be experimented on without adequate anaesthetic or to suffer repeated procedures.[18] The Swedish ladies reported what they had seen to the National Anti-Vivisection Society and their statement was read out at a public meeting in St James's Hall in London.

Bayliss was furious that his reputation had been sullied and he sued the society, winning massive damages. However, the case aroused strong opinions and provoked many articles in the press – some like *The Times* upheld the decision, while others, including *The Daily News,* came out against it. *The Daily News* went on to set up a fund to pay the society's damages and to erect a statue in memory of the little dog. This was sculpted by Joseph Whitehead and erected in the Latchmere estate (one of Britain's first council estates[19]) in Battersea in 1906. The monument took the form of a granite drinking fountain for humans and animals, topped by a brown dog sitting upright, and bearing the inscription:

In Memory of the Brown Terrier Dog done to Death in the Laboratories of University College in February 1903, after having endured

Vivisection extending over more than two months and having been handed from one Vivisector to another till Death came to his Release. Also in Memory of the 232 dogs vivisected at the same place during the year 1902. Men and Women of England, how long shall these things be?

Angry at these developments, resentment grew among local medical students who were so intent on destroying the statue that a police guard had to protect it every night. When the police petitioned Battersea council to contribute to the costs of this protection, Councillor John Archer replied, 'You might as well ask a neighbourhood where burglaries are frequent to pay the expenses of detectives'. Archer, who was a strong supporter of the anti-vivisection movement and London's first black councillor, later became Britain's first black mayor.[18][19][20]

The memorial also became a focus for those demanding improved rights for women and workers. In December 1907, several protests took place with large numbers of medical students marching through London holding effigies of the little brown

FIGURE 17 (opposite): Greater London House in all its art deco, cat-adoring glory.

FIGURE 18: Statue of the little Brown Dog in Battersea Park.

dog and clashing with suffragettes and unionists. One of these so-called Brown Dog Riots turned so violent that 400 police officers had to be brought in to restore order.[20]

In March 1910, frustrated by the controversy and expense, and in spite of demonstrations, injunctions, and a petition with more than 20,000 names, a new Conservative Battersea council removed the little dog and reportedly gave it to a local blacksmith to destroy. It seems that the medical students had won.

However, in 1985, the National Anti-vivisection Society and the British Union for the Abolition of Vivisection donated a new Brown Dog Statue to Battersea Park. Sculpted by Nicola Hicks, and based on her own pet dog, it includes the original statue's inscription while acknowledging the efforts of those still championing the rights of laboratory animals. While very endearing, the little dog is quite different to the first one that sat upright and proud,[21] raising a suggestion that the original message of defiance has been lost.[22]

Certainly, this little statue seems to have had a less fractious time than its predecessor. It enjoys a quiet, some might say hidden, position just north of the English garden section of the park.

DOGS (AND CATS) OF WAR

Over 16 million animals of many kinds served in WWI. They were used for various duties, but also kept as pets and mascots to help boost morale. There's a beautiful memorial to the animals of war in Park Lane and we will visit this and learn about pets in wartime in Chapter 5.

POST-WAR TO THE PRESENT DAY . . . AND BEYOND

With the proliferation of television in the 1940s and 50s came the rise of the pet celeb. Cartoons (like *Tom and Jerry* that first aired in 1940) often featured dogs and cats, with dogs largely portrayed as lovable dolts and cats as having more villainous intentions. Pets feature frequently in films aimed at children and are a big part of the world's longest-running children's

show – *Blue Peter*. One of the first pets to appear in this show, a mongrel called Petra, is commemorated with a bust in the Blue Peter garden.

Today, television viewing is increasingly being replaced by the Internet. Bearing in mind our love of pets and the close bond we have with them, it is perhaps not surprising that they have a strong online presence. What is surprising is just how strong that presence is, especially for cats.

Images of cats are some of the most viewed content on the web and LOLcats – cat pictures superimposed with funny captions often written in 'kittyspeak' – have reached iconic status.

The first cat video was uploaded in 2005 by YouTube co-founder Steve Chen, who posted a clip of his cat, Pajamas, playing with a rope.[23] Ten years later there were over 2 million cat videos on YouTube and the most-watched of these, Nyan cat, has nearly 170 million views. Why do we love cat content so much? Researchers have looked into this and found that the answer is simple: as in real life, seeing cats on the Internet makes us smile.[24]

With all this in mind, it was really only a matter of time before an Internet cat became immortalised as a statue. This honour was extended to a friendly Turkish moggie called Tombili who was caught on camera relaxing in a distinctly laidback pose. Tombili inspired a plethora of popular LOLcat images,[25] but in August 2016 she died after a short illness. This led to over 17,000 people signing a petition to have a monument dedicated to her. This life-size statue, created by local artist Seval Şahin, is in the exact same spot where her iconic photo was taken.

The success of the petition in Istanbul is perhaps not surprising considering the importance of cats in Islamic culture. The prophet Mohammed is said to have cut off the sleeve of his prayer robe rather than disturb his cat, Muezza, who was napping on it. Cats are noted in Islamic teachings for their cleanliness and have long been allowed into mosques.

So, is Tombili the first of many statues dedicated to Internet sensations? Quite possibly. What is for certain is that both dogs and cats are more popular today than at any stage in history. As of 2018, it is estimated that there are 8.9 million dogs in the UK and 11.1 million cats.[26] It doesn't look like this popularity is going to wane anytime soon, so hopefully we can expect to see many more intriguing statues of companion animals adorning our streets and parks.

TOMBILI
Tombili can be found at Zühtüpaşa Mahallesi, Güleç Çk No:1, 34724 Kadıköy/Istanbul. (As an interesting aside, if you visit this location on Google Maps Street View you can actually see the real Tombili here, caught on the Google camera.)

FIGURE 19 (opposite): Tombili striking the pose that brought her Internet fame.

FIGURE 20: Tombili statue with snacks and a slightly surprised street cat.

REFERENCES

1. Bradshaw, J., 2017, *The Science behind Why Some People Love Animals and Others Couldn't Care Less*, Conversation, 28 September.
2. Slezak, M., *Ancient DNA Suggests Dogs Split from Wolves 40,000 Years Ago*, New Scientist, 2016.
3. McMaster, G., *Reading an Ancient Bond in the Look of Puppy Love*, University of Alberta, March 2016.
4. Losey, R.J., *Siberia's Ancient Dog Burials*, Archaeology, March 2016.
5. Pickrell, J., *Oldest Known Pet Cat? 9,500-Year-Old Burial Found on Cyprus*, National Geographic News, April 2004.
6. Beloe, W., *Herodotus, Translated from the Greek, with Notes and Life of the Author*, Thomas Wardle, Philadelphia, 1840.
7. Mark, J.J., *Dogs in the Ancient World*, Ancient History Encyclopedia, June 2014. http://www.ancient.eu/article/184/.
8. Hance, J., *Anubis Not an Egyptian Jackal but African Wolf.* Archaeology News Network, November 2011, https://archaeologynewsnetwork.blogspot.com/2011/01/anubisnot-egyptian-jackal-but-african.html#Kcu2TJ5JbuD8fb1D.99.
9. Hendawi, H., *Egypt Announces Find of Ancient Cat Goddess Temple*, January 2010. Phys.org. http://phys.org/news/201001-egypt-ancient-cat-goddess-temple.html.
10. Grout, G., *Dogs in Ancient Greece and Rome*, Encyclopaedia Romana, http://penelope.uchicago. edu/~grout/encyclopaedia_romana/miscellanea/canes/canes.html.
11. *Molosser Monument 20*, Modern Molosser Magazine, https://modernmolosser.com/articles/jennings-dog/.
12. Williams, D., *Dogged by Debts: The Jennings Dog*, Exploring Ancient Sculpture: Essays in Honour of Geoffrey Waywell, eds. F. MacFarlane and C. Morgan, 225-44, 2010.
13. Abbott, F.R., *Society and Politics in Ancient Rome: Essays and Sketches*, Charles Scribner's Sons, 1912.
14. Wentworth, J.A., and D. Wentworth Blunt-Lytton, *Toy Dogs and Their Ancestors, Including the History and Management of Toy Spaniels, Pekingese, Japanese and Pomeranians*, New York, D. Appleton and company, 1911.
15. About breed standards, The Kennel Club. https://www.thekennelclub.org.uk/services/public/breed/Default.aspx.
16. Governing Council of the Cat Fancy, *The History of Cat Shows*, http://old.gccfcats.org/showcats.html.
17. Carreras Tobacco Company, Wikipedia, https://en.wikipedia.org/wiki/Carreras_Tobacco_Company.
18. Meeke, K., 2009, *The Brown Dog Affair*, Secret London.
19. Mason, *The Brown Dog Affair*, p. 29; Lansbury, Old Brown Dog, p. 13ff.
20. Clough, J., *An Age of Innocence Revisited*, Financial Times, 6 August 2005.
21. You can see an image of the original brown dog statue on the NAVS site: http://www.navs.org.uk/about_us/24/0/286/.
22. Kean., H., 2003, *An Exploration of the Sculptures of Greyfriars Bobby, Edinburgh, and the Brown Dog, Battersea, South London, England*, Society and Animals, 11:4.
23. https://www.youtube.com/watch?v=PvTmxDBxtLs.
24. Dewey, C., 2015, *Comment: The Fascinating, Feel-good Psychology of Internet Cat Videos,* SBS.
25. SukiSury Foto, *Tombili si Kucing 'Meme' Meninggal*, Istanbul, http://chirpstory.com/li/331599.
26. PDSA, 2018, *The PAW Report*, https://www.pdsa.org.uk/get-involved/our-campaigns/pdsa-animal-wellbeing-report.

CHAPTER 2

Till death us do part

LOVE AND LOYALTY

FOR MANY OF US WHO share our homes with cats and dogs, these animals are not just pets, but members of our family. This was neatly demonstrated in a recent study that showed that people often confuse the name of their dog with that of their spouses and children.[1] This, say the researchers, indicates that the dog's name is being pulled from the same cognitive pool as human family members. It seems the same thing happens less with cats, although I have to admit to being guilty of this in the past.

Certainly some pet owners seem to gain the same emotional support from their pets as they might from family. Researchers from Goldsmiths performed a study in which a dog owner and a stranger both sat in a room and performed activities such as humming, speaking, and pretending to cry.[2] Not only did the dogs approach and comfort their owners when they were crying, but they also approached the crying stranger. The humming and speaking stranger, meanwhile, was completely ignored.

This capacity of dogs to lend comfort may explain some of the love we have for them. Research has shown that the ability of dogs and people to communicate, verbally and through gestures, is greater than between any other species.[3] Perhaps this is because we have shared our evolutionary history with them for so long – some 14,000 years – and over this time they have become more and more in tune with our behaviour. It is also said that dogs love us because they think of us as part of their pack and, of course, the success of dogs in the wild would have depended on there being a close bond between pack members.

Cats too communicate with their owners and it seems they are only slightly less successful than dogs at following cues such as pointing. In general, though, their responses to our communications seem less developed. This may be because cats are closer to their wild relatives than dogs are to wolves. The cat ancestor was a solitary hunter, as are all cats with the exception of lions, which works well if you hunt smaller prey by ambush. This difference in hunting styles between cats and dogs helps to explain how our feline friends often lead lives partly independent from ours. It certainly doesn't mean they don't bond with us though. Researchers at the University of Oregon found that most cats prefer social interaction with humans than to a whole range of things including toys, other cats, interesting scents, and food.[4]

There is even biochemical evidence for the shared affection between us and pets. The hormone oxytocin is released in both dog and human brains when we interact and look into each other's eyes.[5] Oxytocin reduces stress and strengthens feelings of affinity, such as those between parents and children. This has led some researchers to surmise that dogs have hijacked our parental bonding responses.

Considering this level of closeness, it is not surprising that we often grieve the loss of our pets. The Blue Cross Pet Bereavement Service received nearly 13,000 calls and emails in 2018 from people seeking support.

Today, we can commemorate the loss of our departed pets in more and more imaginative ways – online memorials, plaster casts of paw prints, even

FIGURE 21: The tombstones at Hyde Park cemetery are mostly arranged in neat rows.

jewellery or tattoos that incorporate our pet's ashes or DNA. Pet burials are popular too, with around forty specialist cemeteries operating in the UK.

But these cemeteries are nothing new. As we saw in Chapter 1, the ancient Egyptians, Greeks, and Romans also buried their pets, and during the 1800s when pet ownership became widespread, pet cemeteries flourished – at least among the wealthy. Visit many stately homes and you will often find pet graves in the grounds. At Fish Cottage in Blockley, Gloucestershire, you can even find a memorial to a pet trout![6]

HYDE PARK PET CEMETERY

Perhaps our best-known Victorian pet cemetery is found at the edge of London's Hyde Park. Down Bayswater Road, not far from the hustle and bustle of Marble Arch, is a special and secret place. Hidden by railings and thick hedges, most people would pass it by without a glance, but peer a little closer and you may catch a glimpse of some of the graves of the pets put to rest here. This little animal necropolis is Hyde Park Pet Cemetery. The cemetery, which started in 1881 and contains at least 475 stones,[7] seems to have come into being after the death of a Maltese terrier called Cherry. Cherry was the much-loved pet of Mr and Mrs Lewis Barned and their children. Living

locally, the Barneds were regular visitors to the park and friends of the gatekeeper at Victoria Lodge, Mr Winbridge, who sold them lollipops and ginger beer. On Cherry's death, the Barneds asked Mr Winbridge if they could bury her in his garden inside the gate. A request he readily accepted.[8]

By all accounts Mr Winbridge was a kindly soul and during the course of the next twenty-two years he devoted more and more of his garden to rows of little tombstones, each marking the resting place of pets that had lived nearby. It is said that the burial ceremony was performed by Winbridge himself, sometimes without the owners present as they were too grief-stricken, other times with family members and canine friends.[8] The graves were well kept and regularly visited.

On a hot, airless day in June 2017, my daughter and I hurried through Hyde Park on our way to meet one of the groundsmen, Clive, who had come over to let us into this bygone world. Clive unlocked the iron gate and there before us were dozens of densely packed, domino-like gravestones, none coming up above our knee and a few just peeking an inch above the grass. Some of the graves were completely hidden beneath the rhododendron bushes that edged the plot, others stood out in full sun. A few were a little drunk in their orientation but many more stood proud.

Interestingly, some of the inscriptions on the tombstones featured names that have stood the test of time pretty well: Sam, Leo, and Rex for example. Others – such as Freaky, Bogie, Smut, and Scum – perhaps less so. The most popular name seems to have been Prince, with Chips, Pippin, and Monty also appearing frequently. Nowadays, we seem to favour human names for our pets.[9] (I know four Lucy's, for example, and three of them are dogs!)

From around the 1850s, human gravestones increasingly bore machine-cut inscriptions that were filled with lead, and that was the case here. Not surprisingly, some of the lead inserts have been lost or eroded by nature, but the vast majority of epitaphs could still be made out, such as: 'In loving memory of my darling little Centi, died March 1893'; '2 faithful black cats – Snow and Smut' (Snow?); 'Darling little Monty who was drowned in old Windsor Lock'; 'Scamp. Run over 29th September 1894.'

'My grandad lost his dog, like that,' Clive told me, nodding towards Scamp's inscription. 'Run over by a horse and cart, he was. Not six miles away.'

It seems to be a fate that befell a fair few of the little dogs interred here.

Clive, my daughter, and I tried to find Cherry's grave, but despite our best efforts (in my case crawling around under bushes) she remained elusive. Most of the pets here had no special claim to fame, save being treasured by their owners, but one held a little notoriety. Clive pointed out his grave – Topper.

Topper sounded a real character. He was apparently a 'common, disreputable fox terrier of "disgraceful habits."'[8] Belonging to Hyde Park Police Station, he would go out on patrol with the officers only to get himself totally lost. He was also 'quite unforgivably greedy', or so it was said, and would make a nuisance of himself around various eating establishments demanding scraps.

I had an hour allocated to look around the cemetery, plenty of time I had thought, but when I checked my watch the hour was almost up. As we headed over to the gate, and, regretfully back to the craziness of the twenty-first century, my daughter noted a little grave marked 'Monkey'. Was this a grave for a real monkey or simply a dog's name? Eric Tourigny who performed a thorough survey of the cemetery's stones is unsure. Monkey was certainly a name given to dogs at the time.

While the graveyard mostly commemorates canines, Dr Tourigny has found at least eight cats. Cat funerals were not unheard of in Victorian times and grieving owners would employ undertakers to build beautiful cat burial baskets and commission clergy to perform special services.[10] Unfortunately, not all members of the public approved, especially if the burial was performed in the consecrated ground of a churchyard. This fact may partly explain why pet cemeteries came into being in the first place. It certainly was a factor in the establishment of our next cemetery, which is in France.

FIGURE 22 (opposite): Memorial stone to Dear Old Spot. In his survey of the cemetery, Eric Tourigny noted that while many graves mentioned loyalty, only a few included Christian symbolism, and though some bore references to a reunion in the afterlife, most avoided explicitly mentioning it. At this time the idea of pets possessing souls was a subject of much controversy. This contrasts with modern cemeteries where the hope of a reunion – illustrated, for example, by the Rainbow Bridge poem and motif, https://en.wikipedia.org/wiki/Rainbow_Bridge_(pets) – is now more socially acceptable. Perhaps reflecting the increasing way animals are viewed as part of the family, modern graves often feature the pet and family name, e.g. Max Buckle.[7]

'It is a space that provides a safe location for humans to convey positive emotion towards this animal-human relationship.'

Hilda Kean on pet cemeteries[12]

HYDE PARK PET CEMETERY
Victoria Gate, Hyde Park, London W2 2UH.
The cemetery is managed by The Royal Parks. At the time of writing, the parks team are planning to offer educational tours of the cemetery. Keep an eye on their website for the next one: https://www.royalparks.org.uk.

PETS IN PARIS

Located a 25-minute metro ride outside Paris, on the banks of the River Seine is the Le Cimetière des Chiens et Autres Animaux Domestiques, or for those of us whose French is a little rusty, the Cemetery of Dogs and Other Domestic Animals. Here is the final resting place for an astonishing 40,000 cats and dogs, not to mention horses, mice, birds, rabbits, a sheep, and a hen.[11] The cemetery opened after a law was passed in 1898 stipulating that pets had to be buried beneath a 'full yard of earth and at least 100 yards from human bodies'.

After paying a small entrance fee, visitors are given a map and may wander freely. Unlike the regular tombstones of Hyde Park cemetery, the graves here come in all shapes and sizes and range from simple unmarked plots to magnificent monuments and marble mausoleums. There are photographs and life-size statues of many of the pets, plus a variety of little stone doghouse tombs. As the cemetery is still in use today, many of the plots are decorated with flowers and favourite playthings such as tennis balls.

Among the graves are a few famous names. There is a monument just inside the entrance to Barry the Saint Bernard, a mountain rescue dog from Switzerland. The tomb's inscription reads rather enigmatically, 'He saved the lives of 40 people. He was killed by the 41st.' The monument shows a small child being carried on the St Bernard's back. This was apparently his forty-first rescue and shortly afterwards poor Barry is reported to have died of exhaustion. However, this is something of a fib and

I am happy to report that Barry lived out his last years comfortably in Bern, dying at the ripe old age of fourteen.

Here is also the resting place of the film star Rin Tin Tin (or Rinty). Rinty was a German shepherd puppy found in a French WWI bombed war-dog kennel. His rescuer was an American corporal named Lee Duncan. Once back in the US, Rinty grew up to be a fine-looking dog who excelled at agility, apparently being able to clear a fence of 11ft 9in.[13] The dog got his first movie break by playing the part of a wolf, as, not surprisingly, he followed instructions better than the real wolf they had been trying to film with. He went on to star in a total of twenty-seven Hollywood movies and his own radio show, greatly boosting the popularity of German shepherds.

On 10 August 1932, Rinty died at Duncan's home in Los Angeles. Devastated, Duncan buried the dog in his own backyard in a bronze casket. However, soon after, he was forced to move due to financial problems. Despite his much-straitened circumstances, when the house was sold Duncan reportedly used some of the proceeds to have Rinty's body returned to his home country for reburial in the Cimetière des Chiens et Autres Animaux Domestiques.

TIDDLES THE CHURCHYARD CAT (1963-80)

Unlike the cats in the Parisian cemetery, tabby cat Tiddles is interred solely among humans. Sid Jacques, verger at St Mary's in Fairford, Gloucestershire, first spotted the little stray when she came to drink from the flower vases in the churchyard.[14] She returned

'Gone for long walkies.'

Inscription on a pet tombstone

FIGURE 23: Cat yawning (or is he laughing?) while sitting on a giant dog statue.

FIGURE 24 (opposite): One of the many cats who have made a home for themselves here in the French cemetery. The cats are fed and cared for by volunteers who have set up a small rescue centre.

each day and was so thin that Sid went over to the local baker to get her some food. That was the start of their seventeen-year relationship.

Tiddles soon made herself at home in the church and became a firm favourite with the congregation, often commandeering peoples' laps during services and occasionally looking out on her flock from the pulpit.

Tiddles was not averse to causing a little mischief too, and one day during the sombre proceedings of a funeral service, she crept unseen beneath the overcoat of one of the mourners, slinking sinuously around his legs and apparently 'nearly frightening the life out of him'.[14]

Her next escapade took place during a festival in which the church proudly displayed its silver. To protect the treasures, a security system was set up and two churchwardens slept over in the church as guards. Suddenly, in the dead of night, the alarms went off, causing the police to rush over and the wardens to have something approaching a heart attack.

Despite a full-scale search of the premises, no intruder was found and everyone was perplexed as to what could have happened. Until, that was, they heard a little meow from above. Tiddles had decided to investigate the security beam and it was she who had set off the alarms.

When Tiddles died, the vicar of St Mary's agreed she could be buried in the churchyard and conducted a special

service for her. Tiddles' grave is marked by a memorial carved by a local stonemason and sits prominently in the churchyard with other town notables.

MORE PET GRAVES AND CEMETERIES – UK
Many of Britain's stately homes feature pet cemeteries and memorials. Below are a few as a taster:
Newstead Abbey (see Chapter 3).
Chartwell (see Chapter 3).
Brahan House Lord Seaforth and his wife are buried in a small cemetery with twenty-one of their dogs. Dingwall, Ross-shire, Scotland IV7 8EE.
Brodsworth Hall Behind the summer house, a path leads to the pets' cemetery where favourite family dogs and even a parrot (Polly) are buried. Home Farm, Doncaster DN5 7XJ. English Heritage.
Edinburgh Castle (see Chapter 3).
Ilford pet cemetery and the Old Blue Cross pet cemetery (see Chapter 5).
Max Gate Thomas Hardy's residence. Hardy and his wife, Emma, created a final resting place for their beloved pets. Most of the headstones were carved by Hardy himself. Look out for the much-loved Wessex, a terrier that loved to bite visitors. Alington Avenue, Dorchester DT1 2AB. National Trust.
Portmeirion Cemetery for the pets of Mrs Adelaide Haig. Adelaide lived in what is now the Portmeirion Hotel until her death in 1917. From accounts it

seems she preferred the company of dogs to humans and would entertain her four-footed friends in the Mirror Room by reading them sermons. Portmeirion Gardens, Portmeirion, Gwynedd, North Wales.

Shugborough At the home of the Earls of Lichfield is a statue of a cat reclining on a vase atop a tall column. The cat is purported to represent one who accompanied Admiral Anson on his journeys around the world. Shugborough, Milford, near Stafford ST17 0XB. National Trust.

Woburn Abbey A pet cemetery and an elaborate Grade II listed monument to the 11th Duchess of Bedford's Pekingese, Che foo (a.k.a. Wuzzy). The Duchess saw her little Che Foo or Wuzzy through rose-tinted specs according to her son, the 12th Duke, who described the animal as 'a most crotchety aggressive little brute'. Woburn Abbey and Gardens, Woburn, Bedfordshire MK17 9WA.

More Pet Graves and Cemeteries –
International

Clara Glen Pet Cemetery Clara and Glen White owned forty-five dogs, dozens of cats, and over 300 rabbits. They started the pet cemetery to bury their own pets, but it now has some 3,800 internments. 2147 Shore Road, Linwood, New Jersey, USA.

Key Underwood Coon Dog Memorial Cemetery Started in 1937 with the burial of the Coon dog, Troop, this cemetery has become a popular tourist attraction and is the only cemetery of its kind in the world. 4945 Coondog Cemetery Road, Cherokee, AL 35616, USA.

Hartsdale Open since 1896 and hence the oldest animal cemetery in the US, it is home to about 80,000 interments. Among the interesting monuments is a huge spaniel mausoleum. 280 Secor Road, Hartsdale, NY 10530, USA.

Los Angeles Pet Memorial Park Founded in 1928, this park includes the gravesites of Hopalong Cassidy's horse, 'Topper'; one of the MGM lions; and other celebrity pets from Hollywood's Golden Age. 5068 Old Scandia Lane, Calabasas, CA 91302, USA.

Jindaiji Pet Cemetery This place of remembrance features compartments that can be rented by pet owners to display jars of their pets ashes along with photos, Buddhist plaques, and pet food. Jindaiji Temple in Chofu City in western Tokyo, Japan.

Guardian angels
Lion

In Victorian times some wealthy pet owners had such a special relationship with their pets that they requested a statue of the animal on their grave. A number of these can be seen in Highgate cemetery, a beautifully eerie, gothic refuge in North London that is famously the resting place of Karl Marx.

THE PARIS PET CEMETERY
Le Cimetière des Chiens et Autres Animaux
Domestiques 4, pont de Clichy, Asnières-sur-Seine,
France. Tél.: 01 40 86 21 11. Train: gare d'Asnières-
sur-Seine. Lignes L et J Bus 540-54.
Open every day except Mondays.
16 March to 15 October – 10am to 6pm. 16 October
to 15 March – 10am to 4:30pm. Closed on public
holidays, except on 1 November. Charge – 3.50 euros.

TIDDLES THE CHURCHYARD CAT
St Mary's church, Fairford, Gloucestershire, GL7 4AF.

Figure 25: Tiddles'
commemorative tombstone.

Highgate is probably the best known of the so-called garden cemeteries, which are seven park-like graveyards built in a ring around London. These cemeteries, known as The Magnificent Seven, were commissioned by parliament during the first half of the nineteenth century when the population of London more than doubled to 2.3 million. Such a surge in numbers was causing a serious lack of burial space in the churchyards and the sort of sanitary problems not seen since the Plague.

Highgate cemetery is divided into east and west sections, and in the latter you can take a guided tour that includes a visit to the Grade II listed tomb of the world's first heavyweight boxing champion, Tom Sayers.

On a sunny day in June when I took the tour, our knowledgeable guide noted how it was strange to think that someone like Tom Sayers who was incredibly famous in his time is now almost unheard of, at least unless you are acquainted with the history of boxing.

Born in Brighton in 1826, Sayers grew up unable to read, write, or tell the time, but what he lacked in learning he certainly made up for in courage and strength. His sport was bare-knuckle boxing, a brutal and illegal occupation that makes today's UFC fights look decidedly tame.

Sayer's most famous fight took place on 17 April 1860 in a field in Farnborough, Hampshire. Watched by thousands, including Charles Dickens and then Prime Minister Lord Palmerston, it was against a much larger opponent from America – John Carmel Heenan, who had made a name for himself fighting in San Francisco's docklands. The battle lasted two and a half hours before it was finally brought to an end by local police storming the field. By this stage both fighters were terribly beaten up. Heenan was blinded in both eyes and Sayers had veins hanging from his arms. The fight caused a sensation, both here and in America, and Sayers was declared a national hero. However, his adoring fans were desperate for him to retire and a public subscription of £3,000 was raised so that he could do just that. His fighting days over, Sayers travelled the country in style and was often seen riding in a carriage through Camden with his loyal pet mastiff, Lion, who rarely left his side.

When Sayers died of consumption in 1865, the same year the Queensberry Rules for boxing were introduced, thousands lined the streets of Camden to march with his body to Highgate. It was, our tour guide believes, the largest funeral procession ever to have taken place in London up to that time. The cortège was led by Lion, and, according to a newspaper report: 'The dog, with "a band of crape" around his neck, behaved impeccably. Not so the other spectators at the cemetery, who "danced and screamed, yelled and hooted, whistled and shrieked, like demons."'[15]

FIGURE 26: A lovely dog sits on the grave of the Gardiner family, just inside the East cemetery.

FIGURE 27: A little cat (the only one I could find in Highgate) adorned this grave. The open-book headstone is thought to represent the book of life or Bible.

Lion lived three years after his owner and his likeness lies on Tom's tomb. With his head resting on crossed paws, he looks forever peaceful, if not a little melancholic, in his wonderfully leafy oasis.

Mrs Chippy

On the other side of the world in New Zealand, we find a no less charming pet guarding his owner's grave, Mrs Chippy.

Mrs Chippy was a passenger on Ernest Shackleton's ship, the *Endurance*, which set sail from London in 1914 on the Trans-Antarctic expedition. On this mission Shackleton hoped to be the first person to cross the Antarctic continent on foot.

Mrs Chippy belonged to Henry McNish, the ship's carpenter (or chippy as they were known) and followed his owner wherever he went – a fact that didn't escape the crew who came up with the tabby's name. The moniker is a little misleading, however, as Mrs Chippy was actually a tough Glaswegian tom.[16.]

In one of the crew's many diaries from the trip, the cat was described by the men as being 'full of character', and it is likely that he was actually more popular than his owner, McNish, who was gruff and surly, though well respected as a sailor and shipwright.

In her book documenting the cat's many adventures, Caroline Alexander relates how Mrs Chippy would take delight in leaping across the kennels of the sledging dogs, just out of reach.[17] One can imagine the roar of barking that would have gone up, for there were some sixty-nine dogs aboard, a mixture of wolf and large breeds such as collies, bloodhounds, retrievers, and Newfoundlands.[16]

It seems Mrs Chippy used up a lot of his nine lives on the voyage. Once, after he fell overboard, the ship had to be turned around so he could be scooped out of the freezing waters with the biologist's net. On another occasion, the ship's bosun, who was clearly more a dog person, was annoyed at Mrs Chippy taunting the dogs and would have thrown him to the pack had not one of the crew, Perce Blackborrow, stopped him. Such was the affection for the cat that the bosun was severely reprimanded for his actions.

In January 1915, when less than 100 miles from their destination harbour, the *Endurance* became entrapped in the frozen Weddell Sea. The crew awaited a thaw for many months, but on 27 October 'the stout little ship' could live up to her name no longer, and the pressure of the ice finally caused her to break up and be lost to the ocean.

The men were forced to camp out on the ice for a further six months. In April, with winter fast approaching, Shackleton decided they would have to use the three lifeboats and make their way to the nearest land, some 350 miles away. He ordered that they could only take essential items with them – an understandable decision, but one with

FIGURE 28 (opposite): The grave of Thomas Sayers with his ever-faithful mastiff, Lion.

FIGURE 29: Perce Blackborow on board ship with Mrs Chippy, McNish's cat, on his shoulder.

heart-breaking consequences for the expedition's animals. In his diary, the ship's photographer, Frank Hurley, recorded it as follows: 'This afternoon Sallie's three youngest pups; Sue's Sirius; and [Mrs] Chippy, the carpenter's cat, have to be shot. We could not undertake maintenance of weaklings under the new conditions. Macklin, Crean and the carpenter seemed to feel the loss of their friends rather badly.'[17]

The crew eventually made it to the deserted and wind-blasted Elephant Island, but with no chance of rescue there, Shackleton was forced to lead a team of five men on towards South Georgia where there was a whaling station. This trip of 800 miles in a 22ft open boat over some of the world's most treacherous seas has been described as one of the most astonishing journeys ever made. One of those chosen for this perilous trip was McNish who somehow managed to adapt the little boat to enable it to withstand the extreme conditions.

After safely reaching South Georgia, a ship was sent to rescue the remaining men back on Elephant Island. Mercifully, all were still alive although many were in very poor health. Historians believe that without McNish's skills the boat would never have made it to Georgia. Despite this, Shackleton did not put the carpenter forward for the Polar Medal, a commendation given to all but four of the crew. McNish had fallen out with Shackleton at numerous times on the voyage and never forgave him for shooting his cat, Mrs Chippy.

In the 1920s, McNish went to work on the waterfront in Wellington, New Zealand. The curator of Antarctic History at the Canterbury Museum in Christchurch met McNish in his later years. 'The only thing I remember him saying,' he recalls, 'was that Shackleton shot his cat.'[18]

After he died in 1930, McNish was honoured with a naval funeral, yet his grave stayed unmarked until 1959 when the New Zealand Antarctic Society erected a headstone. Then, in 2004, McNish and his much-loved cat were finally reunited. A life-size bronze statue of Mrs Chippy by the sculptor Chris Elliott was placed on the grave by the New Zealand Antarctic Society.

McNish's grandson, Tom, who lives in Norwich said, 'If it wasn't for him they would all have perished. His skills got them to safety. But all you hear about the expedition is Shackleton. I think he would be over the moon about the statue. The cat was more important to him than the Polar Medal.'[19]

FOREVER FAITHFUL?

As you might expect, there are many tales of dogs exhibiting loyalty to their owners. While researching these I found the accounts would often vary and it is not beyond the realms of possibility that some have been embellished over time to create a more compelling narrative. In a few cases the authenticity of the tale has been completely debunked (see Greyfriars Bobby – Chapter 6). Certainly, the

devotion of dogs is evident in tales where they remain in the area their owners passed away. However, once the time they stay stretches to years, it's likely to be because they've been receiving food and attention in these places, rather than due to extreme fidelity. In other words, dogs are loyal but not stupid! With these caveats in mind, here are a few well-loved tales of canine loyalty that have been commemorated with statues.

Hachiko (Hachi)

Hachiko's tale begins in 1924 when Hideamuro Ueno, a professor at Tokyo University, became his owner. Every morning Hachiko would watch Ueno leave for work and every afternoon at 4pm he would wait at the Shibuya Train Station in central Tokyo for his master's return. This continued for almost two years, until, on 21 May 1925, Hachiko's owner never showed up, having suffered a fatal stroke while at work.

After the untimely demise of his owner, Hachiko was adopted by a friend of the lecturer, but every day for the rest of his ten-year life he would return to the Shibuya Train Station at 4pm, awaiting his owner.

Soon the press picked up the story and Hachiko became a national celebrity, leading to a huge boost in the popularity of Akitas. Teachers and parents taught the tale to their children as an example

of family loyalty and even Emperor Hirohito is supposed to have appropriated the story in pre-War Japan to inspire fidelity-to-the-end amongst his people.

In 1935, Shibuya Station held a ceremony for their famous resident, unveiling a bronze statue in his honour, but sadly, less than a year later, the dog was found dead in a nearby street, having died of cancer.

A bronze Hachiko still sits outside the station (the original was melted down for metal during WWII), and the station also features a large and colourful wall mosaic devoted to the dog. Both continue to attract large numbers of Hachiko fans.

Over the years, this famous Akita has featured in several films, including the box office hit *Hachi: A Dog's Tale*. (Be sure to have a hanky ready if you watch it.) He has also appeared in books, advertising campaigns, and even an episode of the US cartoon *Futurama*. And in 2003 when a new community minibus was brought to the area, what else could they name it but the Hachiko-bus?

Perhaps most touching was the installation in 2015 of a new statue to Hachiko at the University of Tokyo, marking the 80th anniversary of his death. And if you find the solitary Hachiko at the station a little sad, then you will no doubt be happy to find him reunited with his owner at last, in the grounds of the university.

MRS CHIPPY

Mrs Chippy, Karori Cemetery, 76 Old Karori Road, Wellington, 6012, New Zealand.

HACHIKO

Original statue: Shibuya station, 1 Chome-2 Dogenzaka, Shibuya, Tokyo 150-0043, Japan.

Statue with Ueno: Dept. of Agriculture, University of Tokyo, Yayoi campus. 7-3-1, Hongo, Bunkyo-ku, Tokyo, Japan.

FIGURE 30 (opposite) : The statue of Mrs Chippy that was added to McNish's grave.

FIGURE 31: The first Hachiko statue situated outside Shibuya Railway Station makes a nice place for a local cat to take a nap.

Ruswarp

Here in the UK we have our own stories of canine loyalty, including one that is an affecting tale of railways, wild places, and a very devoted border collie.

The Settle to Carlisle railway travels through some breathtakingly beautiful landscapes in the Yorkshire Dales and Cumbrian Fells. It has been described as one of the world's greatest railways and yet it was threatened with closure during the 1980s. Many opposed this and a petition against it soon amassed thousands of signatures, including a paw print from a dog called Ruswarp. Ruswarp (pronounced Russup) belonged to Graham Nuttall, a founding member of the Friends of the Settle-Carlisle Line, which thankfully managed to save the service.

On 20 January 1990, Graham bought day return tickets to Llandrindod Wells in the Welsh mountains where he planned to do some hiking. However, it soon became apparent that man and dog had not returned from their trip. The alarm was raised and police searches made, but to no avail.

Then on 7 April, nearly three months after Graham had set out on his walk, his body was found by another walker next to a mountain stream. Beside him was Ruswarp. The fourteen-year-old collie had stayed with his master through snow, wind, and rain for eleven weeks. The dog was so weakened by his ordeal that he had to be carried down from the mountain.

Sadly, despite being given the greatest of care by a local vet, Ruswarp died shortly after attending his master's funeral. But Ruswarp and Graham would not be forgotten. In 2009, twenty years after the line's reprieve and as a way to commemorate Ruswarp's incredible loyalty, a bronze statue was installed at Garsdale Station.[20]

At the unveiling, Mark Rand, chairman of the Friends of the Settle to Carlisle Line, poignantly recalled how important Graham and Ruswarp had been in keeping the service open:

> A petition objecting to the closure was signed by 32,000 people and one dog. That dog was Ruswarp who had his say with a paw print. Today the railway line is thriving again. Having a statue there of Ruswarp will symbolise not only the successful fight to save the line but also the loyalty of man's best friend.[21]

MORE FAITHFUL DOGS

Greyfriars Bobby (see Chapter 6).

Charles Gough A talented young artist, Gough was killed by a fall in the Lake District in 1805. In a story reminiscent of Ruswarp, his dog, Foxie, remained where he fell for three months. The spot is marked with a memorial stone inscribed with poems on the fidelity of dogs by Wordsworth and Sir Walter Scott. Charles Gough Memorial, Helvellyn, Cumbria.

FIGURE 32: Hachiko and his owner meet again in the grounds of the University of Tokyo.

Tip stayed with his master when he died on Howden Moor in Derbyshire for fifteen weeks through one of the area's harshest winters. West tower of Derwent dam, Peak District National Park, England.

Dzok (pronounced as Jock) waited at the Rondo Grunwaldzkie roundabout in Kraków, Poland, to be fetched by his master who had died there. Find Dzok a few minutes from the Castle's Dragon. Vistula Walkway, Kraków, Poland.

Kostya was a passenger in a car that was involved in a collision in which his owners both died. He is said to have remained at the intersection where they were killed for the rest of his life. His statue was the first non-political one erected in the region. Lev Yashin Street, Togliatti, Russia.

Karina and Naido When four-year-old Karina became lost in the Siberian wilderness, her German shepherd puppy, Naido, stayed with her, keeping her warm for nine days. In 2015, a statue was unveiled at the local airport. Yakutsk airport, Sakha Republic, Russia.

Old Shep is said to have maintained a five-and-a-half-year vigil for his master at a railway station in Fort Benton, Montana, after his owner died in the area. A lovely bronze monument to Shep, showing him looking out across the river with his two front paws on a railway track, was created in 2014. A nice touch is that members of the public may purchase memorial bricks for their own departed pets that are set round the statue's base. Fort Benton, Montana, USA (see figure 4).

An interview with
JOEL WALKER, RUSWARP SCULPTRESS

What were the challenges with this commission?
Part of the difficulty and challenge of the Ruswarp project was the small number of photographs that I had to work from and only a few reported eyewitness accounts of what he was like. I did have several key newspaper images and a very important clip from his appearance in a documentary made about the saving of the Settle to Carlisle line.

What were the physical characteristics of Ruswarp you most wanted to capture?
He was a neat tricolour collie, sometimes described as Irish in type. He carried his ears high and slightly tipped over. He did not have a large ruff, nor was he smooth coated. He had a special 'bib' of hair high on his chest under his throat and a coat that varied in texture – with waves and length on his front legs and collie 'trousers'. I loved his plumy tail and the character that you could see even in the brief moments as he got onto the train with his human Graham Nuttall.

And what about his pose and expression?
The statue needed to sum up a lot of history, feeling, and emotion. It was important that Ruswarp should look as if he was on guard. I felt that if he was shown to be sitting, it reflected his

remaining with Graham for eleven weeks – his loyalty. Yet he also appears ready to get up and go at any moment. Ruswarp the statue is gazing out across the railway they helped save and over the countryside they loved.

Can you tell us a little bit about the stages you went through creating the statue?
After a spring trip to Garsdale Station, a site for the statue was suggested and from this, the pose for Ruswarp was developed. By the summer, progress had been made building up the main armature and forming the body. I had assistance from local collie owners, all of whom were very helpful with visits, photographs, and feedback. This helped me achieve the details of physicality and conformation that go to make a 'collie dog' – the neat shapes of paws, quickness of eye, and sense of athleticism. I worked through the autumn and into January to finalise the details of the coat and finish the expression. At last, with permission from the representatives of the commissioners (the Friends of the Settle to Carlisle Line headed up by Mark Rand, who was chairman at the time), we had a visit from the mould-maker to make the mould of the statue. Then it was time to go through the foundry process and finish the wax stage. After all this was done there was the installation at Garsdale!

FIGURE 33: Joel adds detail to Ruswarp's coat.

FIGURE 34: Ruswarp meets a few collie friends.

FIGURE 35: Ruswarp surveying his favourite station
(Garsdale railway station, Yorkshire Dales National Park, Sedbergh LA10 5PP).

REFERENCES
1. Deffler, S.A., Fox, C., Ogle, C.M. and D.C. Rubin, 2016, *All My Children: The Roles of Semantic Category and Phonetic Similarity in the Misnaming of Familiar Individuals, Memory and Cognition*, 44(7), pp.989-99.
2. Custance, D.M. and J. Mayer, 2012, *Empathic-like Responding by Domestic Dogs* (Canis familiaris) t*o Distress in Humans: An Exploratory Study*, Animal Cognition, 15(5), pp.851-9.
3. Udell, M.A. and C.D.K. Wynne, 2008, *A Review of Domestic Dogs'* (Canis Familiaris) *Human-like Behaviors: Or Why Behavior Analysts Should Stop Worrying and Love Their Dogs,* 89(2), pp.247-61.
4. Vitale Shreve, K.R., Mehrkam, L.R. and M.A.R. Udell, 2017, *Social Interaction, Food, Scent or Toys? A Formal Assessment of Domestic Pet and Shelter Cat* (Felis silvestris catus) *Preferences,* 141(3), pp.322-8.
5. Nagasawa, M., Kikusui, T., Onaka, T. and M. Ohta, 2009, *Dog's Gaze at Its Owner Increases Owner's Urinary Oxytocin during Social Interaction,* 55(3), pp.434-441.
6. Lambton, L., 1986, *Beastly Buildings: The National Trust Book of Architecture for Animals,* Historic England Publishing.
7. Tourigny, E., Lecturer in Historical Archaeology at Newcastle University, Personal communication.
8. The Strand magazine. 1893, *A Cemetery for Dogs*. London.
9. Rover.com blog – https://www.rover.com/blog/100most-popular-male-female-dog-names-2016.
10. Matthews, M., 2016, *Cat Funerals in the Victorian Era* – https://www.mimimatthews.com.
11. O'Hare, S., *Pets in Peace: World's Oldest Pet Cemetery Where a Lion and a Racehorse Are among 40,000 Bodies is Discovered in Paris*, Daily Mail, 15 January 2013.
12. Kean., H. 2013, *Human and Animal Space in Historic 'Pet' Cemeteries in London, New York and Paris*, Animal Death, eds. Johnson, J., Probyn-Rapsey, F., Sydney University Press.
13. Bondeson, J., 2011, *Amazing Dogs: A Cabinet of Canine Curiosities*, Cornell University Press.
14. Lewis-Jones, J., 2001, *Voices of Fairford and Lechlade*, History Press, Stroud.
15. Sonin, A., *Heritage: Victorian Bricklayer Tom Sayers Became World's First Heavyweight Boxing Champion*, Ham and High, 19 October 2013.
16. Alexander, C., 1999, *Mrs Chippy's Last Expedition*, Harper Perennial, London.
17. Alexander, C., 1998, *The Endurance: Shackleton's Legendary Antarctic Expedition*, Bloomsbury.
18. *Antarctic Hero 'Reunited' with Cat,* BBC, http://news.bbc. Co.uk/1/hi/sci/tech/3818613.stm.
19. Chapman, P., *Tribute to Cat Killed by Shackleton in Antarctic*, The Telegraph, 28 June 2004.
20. Walker, J., *Ruswarp: The Story and Sculpture,* 12 May 2008, http://ruswarp.blogspot.co.uk.
21. Harvey, M., *The Statue of Ruswarp in Memory of Graham Nuttall,* Friends of the Settle-Carlisle Line, http://www.foscl.org.uk/content/history/statue-ruswarp-memory-grahamnuttall.

CHAPTER 3

Love me, love my pet

POLITICS, ROYALTY AND SCIENCE

IN 2008, SOME PSYCHOLOGISTS performed an experiment in which an attractive Frenchman approached random women to see if they'd like to go on a date. On half these approaches he took his little dog along with him.[1] The idea was to see if the dog improved his chances – and the answer was a resounding yes! Only 10 per cent of women agreed when the man was alone, whereas three times that many did when he was joined by his dog.

The same researchers also tested whether people are more likely to give to beggars if they have dogs. Interestingly, the results were very similar. When a stranger asked people for money, 11 per cent obliged when he was alone, whereas 35 per cent did so when he was *avec le chien*.

Studies such as these suggest that people such as politicians (and maybe estate agents and tax collectors) who hope to endear themselves to the public could do worse than be seen with a friendly dog. It was a tactic that worked well for Richard Nixon. Just ahead of the US elections in 1952, Nixon was accused of receiving illegal campaign funds. It seemed a foregone conclusion that he would resign. Nixon decided to play one last card, however. He appeared on TV and contritely admitted to being terribly in debt. He went on to say that despite his financial woes and the fact that he would have to give many things up, there was one thing he could never part with – his little girl's pet spaniel, Checkers. Nixon astutely appealed to both our love of dogs and of family, and his popularity rocketed. Perhaps it's not surprising, then, that almost every US president

has had a dog.[2] (Although, as of time of writing, Donald Trump does not and, according to his first wife, Ivana, is 'not a dog fan'.)

A 2012 study investigated this phenomenon further with an in-depth look at the use of pets as public relations tools by US presidents.[3] They found that in times of war or scandal, dogs were featured in more public appearances than in periods of economic hardship. The theory was that pets were a 'reassuring presence' during times of conflict, but likely to trigger resentment in periods of austerity.

What about cats? Do they have a similar effect on our collective consciousness, or are dog and cat owners perceived differently? The answer to the latter is quite possibly. Studies seem to suggest that those who self-identify as 'cat people' may have different personality traits to those identifying as 'dog people'. Research into the social media profiles of both found that cat owners tend to experience the emotions of anxiety, depression, and vulnerability more acutely than dog owners and have more reserved and reflective personalities. Dog owners seem to be more extroverted and friendly, however they are also more conscientious and less open to new experiences and adventures.[4]

Perhaps it is best to cover all bases and have both types of pet, as the Clintons did with Socks, their black-and-white moggie, and Buddy, their chocolate Labrador. What is almost beyond doubt is that cats and dogs help people appear more relatable. When we see a person in authority stroking a cat or walking their dog, it makes that

person seem more like us – someone who gets fur and drool on their clothes, who empties litter trays and picks up poo.

Poodle Spirit

Whether Churchill thought having his dog with him during WWII would reassure the public, we will never know, but certainly he was often seen with the miniature brown poodle, Rufus, by his side. Sadly, the little dog was killed in a traffic accident while still young, but the famous statesman soon obtained another curly companion, the aptly named Rufus II, who lived to the impressive age of fifteen.

Churchill was a great lover of all animals and had a veritable menagerie at his home, Chartwell, in Kent. The non-human cast of characters included horses, cows, fish, pigs, dogs, and black swans.

In 2012, more than 800,000 of Churchill's papers, including many letters that he wrote home, were made available online.[5] In these letters he would always send love to each of the pets in turn. In one letter, written while Churchill was at school in Harrow, he asks his mother's permission to exchange his bicycle for a bulldog called Dodo, whom he noted was very true and affectionate – she refused.[6] Later correspondence show how distraught he was when Rufus II was unwell.

Along with all the other animals, there were many cats at Chartwell too, including a large tabby called Mickey. Mickey was once playing with the telephone cord while Churchill was on a call to the Lord Chancellor. Churchill reputedly yelled, 'Get off the line you fool!', before having to assure the Lord Chancellor that he hadn't meant him.

Towards the end of his life, Churchill was given a ginger cat with white chest and socks as a birthday present from his private secretary, Jock Colville. Churchill was very fond of the cat, whom he named Jock after his secretary, and would take him along when he travelled between Chartwell and his London home in Hyde Park Gate. The last photograph of Churchill in parliament shows the marmalade cat in the background.

After Churchill died in 1965, Chartwell was given by Churchill's family to the National Trust to care for in perpetuity. However, the family made a special request. They asked that a marmalade cat with white bib and socks should always be resident at the house. The National Trust have kept this promise and the latest Jock in residence, Jock VI, was a rescue kitten from the animal shelter, Croydon Animal Samaritans.

In the summer of 2017, my daughter and I went to visit this lucky cat and talk to Katherine Barnett,

FIGURE 37: Jock poses by a bust of his benefactor.

FIGURE 36 (opposite): Churchill leaving 10 Downing Street in August 1953 with his VIP or Very Important Poodle – Rufus II.

House and Collections Manager at Chartwell. Having visited the grounds of this house as a National Trust member many times, it was fun to go up to the big front door and ring the doorbell like so many important people must have done in the past. We were welcomed into the Secretary's Room and there, armed with camera and a bag of salmon Dreamies, we awaited the arrival of this special cat.

Jock was brought in, nestled in Katherine's arms. He was a slim-built, friendly individual with an amusing little white moustache. Of course, he was ginger with a white chest and white legs – just as Churchill would have wanted. As Jock VI devoured Dreamies and leapt around on the sofa (hopefully not digging his claws in too much), Katherine spoke about how fond Churchill was of his feline friends. Some might even conclude he was rather obsessive, especially about the original Jock, who had to be seated at the table in a special place before the family could even think about beginning their evening meal. Jock was even a guest at Churchill's grandson's wedding.

Katherine also recalled a story about what happened when one of Churchill's other cats was lost for three days after being shouted at. Churchill felt so guilty at raising his voice that he put a note in the window requesting forgiveness and asking that the cat come home forthwith. A couple of hours later that's exactly what happened.

The affection Churchill shared with his felines remained right to the end. It is said that the first Jock was resting on his bed when the great man finally passed away in January 1965, aged ninety. Jock the first then lived out the rest of his life at Chartwell and all the subsequent Jocks have been rescue cats.

'When a new one is recruited it often causes a bit of a stir,' Katherine explained. 'When the current Jock took up residence, he was featured in some 500 press stories and made the papers as far away as *The Sydney Morning Herald* in Australia.'

'And is he popular with the staff and visitors?' I asked.

'Oh, everyone is very fond of him,' Katherine said. 'His tweets are the most liked on the National Trust's twitter account and many people are keen to meet him. We had someone come all the way from Arkansas in the US once, especially to see him.'

Certainly Jock's story is one of rags to riches. Katherine goes on to explain how he was originally found, aged six months, living rough in a shed in Croydon. He was underweight and his ginger fur was matted with red paint. Not the most auspicious of starts.

CHARTWELL
Chartwell, Mapleton Road, Westerham TN16 1PS.
Owned by National Trust. Admission charge.

'Dogs are great assets to candidates, and the feeling seems to be engendered that if a dog loves the candidate, he can't be all that bad.'

Dick Gregory

Now he is living it up in a grand stately home with over eighty acres to roam in, plus the company of several other moggies, should he wish it, who live in the cottages on the estate.

Jock obligingly poses for a few photos and then it is time for us to depart. If you visit Chartwell you can see the graves of Rufus, Rufus II, and the original Jock in the gardens. And if you are lucky you may also spot the latest Jock somewhere too – a living link to the past of this special place.

ROOSEVELT AND THE FIRST DOG, FALA

In the summer of 1941, Churchill met with President Roosevelt aboard the *USS Augusta*. The purpose of the meeting was to sign the Atlantic Charter that aimed to strengthen relations between the two countries. It was likely a rather serious meeting so it was lucky that there was a little dog there to lighten the mood. This was Fala, the president's much-loved Scottish terrier.

Fala was given to Roosevelt as a puppy in the autumn of 1940 by his cousin Mary Suckley. Originally called Big Boy, the president renamed the pup Murray the Outlaw of Falahill after a Scottish ancestor, but this being a bit of a mouthful, it was soon shortened to Fala. The little dog worked his way into the president's heart almost immediately. Every night he would sleep in a dedicated chair at the foot of Roosevelt's bed and every morning there was a bone for him on the president's breakfast tray.

Fala was popular with White House staff too, especially those of the kitchen where he was a frequent visitor. Soon he became very overweight and was diagnosed with intestinal problems due to all the exotic titbits he'd been given. After this, Roosevelt laid down the law: 'Not one CRUMB will be fed to Fala except by the president!' he declared.

Roosevelt had contracted polio in his thirties that had led to him being paralysed from the waist down. His illness necessitated many trips to the doctors and he would often take Fala along. The dog accompanied him on official visits too, including one to the Aleutian Islands where it was rumoured that he was accidentally left behind. During the 1944 presidential campaign, the Republicans accused Roosevelt of wasting millions of dollars of taxpayers' money in sending a ship to the islands to retrieve the dog. This led to the president making one of his best-known and most-loved speeches. In the so-called Fala Speech, he notes, 'I am accustomed to hearing malicious falsehoods about myself and I do not resent them. . . . But I think I have a right to object to libellous statements about my dog.' He goes on to say that Fala's Scotch soul was furious at the Republicans' unfounded accusations![7] The audience were up on their feet, laughing, and cheering, and Roosevelt was duly re-elected for an unprecedented fourth term.

By now everyone knew and loved Fala. He had endeared himself to the nation with his jaunty looks and his loyalty to the president; not to mention an impressive array of tricks, such as standing on his back legs whenever the 'Star-Spangled Banner' was played. The dog received so much fan mail that a secretary was employed just to deal with it.

Towards the end of the war Roosevelt grew increasingly frail, and in April 1945 he died unexpectedly from a massive stroke while at his home in Georgia. It is said that when he passed away Fala became very agitated, crashing through a screen door and running to the top of a nearby hill where he sat howling.

The little dog lived out the rest of his life with Mrs Eleanor Roosevelt in the country at Val-Kill. Eleanor brought Fala's grandson, Tamas, to keep Fala company and they would often run off together, coming home much later, caked in mud and covered with burrs. However, the former first lady recalled in her biography how the dog still pined for his master:

Fala always lay near the dining-room door where he could watch both entrances just as he did when his master was there. Franklin would often decide suddenly to go somewhere and

PARLIAMENTARY CATS

While Churchill was prime minister, there were three felines living at Number 10: Peter, Nelson, and Peter II. In fact, there seems to have been a Treasury or Downing Street moggie since way back in 1515 when Cardinal Wolsey brought his cat along to meetings with Henry VIII (see Chapter 1).

Little is known of the early cats, but in 2005, documents were made public that revealed the names of parliamentary cats dating from 1929 onwards. Back in the 1920s it had been declared by the Treasury that money from the petty cash could be set aside for the maintenance of an 'efficient cat'. A rather euphemistic way of saying one that could rid parliament of its copious mice and rats.

As of 2018 there are no fewer than five cats on Whitehall mouse patrol – Evie and Ossie of the Cabinet Office, Palmerston at the Foreign and Commonwealth Office, and Gladstone at the Treasury. Perhaps the most important, though, at least if his grand title is anything to go by, is Larry who is Chief Mouser to the Cabinet Office and resident at Number 10.

Larry's story is another of those rags-to-riches tales – let no one tell you that there are no opportunities for social mobility in Britain! In February 2011, he was one of many rescue cats being cared for at Battersea Dogs and Cats Home, and maybe he would have stayed there a while longer had not a rat been seen scuttling across the steps of Number 10 during a live ITV news report.

Spurred into action by this public display of a pest predicament, then Prime Minister David Cameron and his family sought out Larry who was reputed to be an excellent mouser (though rumour has it that his ability in this area may have been overstated).[9]

At any rate, Larry appears to be taking parliamentary life in his stride, surviving two cabinet reshuffles. According to the Official Downing Street website: 'Larry spends his days greeting guests to the house, inspecting security defences and testing antique furniture for napping quality. His day-to-day responsibilities also include contemplating a solution to the mouse occupancy of the house. Larry says this is still "in tactical planning stage."'

Inexplicably, no one has yet created a monument to any of these feline civil servants, but you can see a fine blue plaque dedicated to Larry, near his former pen at Battersea Dogs and Cats Home.

FIGURE 38: Larry looking like the cat who got the cream, outside Number 10.

You can follow the current parliamentary cats on twitter:
Larry - @Number10cat (unofficial)
Palmerston -@DiploMog
Gladstone - @TreasuryMog (unofficial)
Evie - @HMCabinetCat (unofficial)

Fala had to watch both entrances in order to be ready to spring up and join the party on short notice. Fala accepted me after my husband's death, but I was just someone to put up with until the master should return.[8]

Fala died in 1952 and was buried at the foot of Roosevelt's grave.

Lincoln and Animal Rights

Another president who was known for his empathy towards animals and who seemed quite ahead of his time in this regard was Abraham Lincoln. Lincoln was the sixteenth president of the United States and was in office from 1861 until his assassination in 1865.

From an early age, Lincoln seems to have spoken up against animal cruelty and unlike many frontiersmen he was not a fan of hunting. In his book about the president, Matthew Algeo quotes Lincoln's reaction when the piglet he'd been keeping as a pet had to be killed:

I saw the hog, dressed, hanging from the pole near the barn. I began to blubber. I just couldn't reconcile myself to my loss. I could not stand it, and went far back into the woods again, where I found some nuts that satisfied my hunger till night, when I returned home. They could not get me to take any of the meat; neither tenderloin, nor sausage, nor souse; and even months after, when the cured ham came on the table, it made me sad and sick to look at it.[11]

Lincoln is also famous for owning cats and dogs. His wife noted, possibly with a wry smile, that adopting kittens was almost a hobby for him and Lincoln is said to have found playing with his cats helpful in dealing with the stresses of the day.

Similarly, a dog appears to have assisted the president in coping with depression. Around 1855 when he was in his forties, Lincoln adopted a stray mutt that he found near his home in Springfield, Illinois. He named the dog Fido, which in Latin is translated as 'to trust, believe, and confide in', and living up to that name, Fido followed his master everywhere.[12]

When he was elected president, Lincoln made the difficult decision to leave Fido with his lifelong friends at Springfield, along with the dog's favourite

ROOSEVELT AND FALA MEMORIAL
Franklin Delano Roosevelt Memorial, 1850 West
Basin Dr SW, Washington, DC 20242, USA.

ABRAHAM LINCOLN
See Lincoln and his dog (Abraham Lincoln the
Hoosier Youth) in front of the Lincoln Life Insurance
Office, 1300 South Clinton Street, Fort Wayne,
Indiana 46802, USA. You can also see Lincoln with a
pig on W. Main Cross Street, Taylorville, Illinois, USA.

'I care not for a man's religion whose dog
and cat are not the better for it.'

Abraham Lincoln

FIGURE 39 (opposite): Roosevelt's statue is made all the
more special by the addition of his little dog.

FIGURE 40: Lincoln as a youth with his dog by his side.

horsehair sofa. He and his sons loved the dog a great
deal, but Lincoln felt that the journey to Washington
and his hectic new life at the White House would be
too much for Fido, who was of a nervous disposition.

There were some strict rules for Fido's new owners.
They were under instruction never to leave the dog
tied up in the yard or to scold him for muddy paws.
He was to be allowed inside whenever he scratched
at the door and he was to be given scraps from the
dining room table every day. This, we may remember,
was at a time when many dogs could be treated
roughly, partly due to the fact that they could carry
diseases like rabies.

In his book, Algeo argues that Lincoln's empathy for
creatures may well have been reflected in his politics.
Certainly he was seen as a compassionate man who
paved the way towards the abolition of slavery and
who pardoned Union Army deserters. Amongst his
famous quotes are many that speak of his regard for
animals and of his strong belief in kindness.

MORE POLITICAL PET STATUES
Downtown Rapid City Here you can view The City
of Presidents, a series of life-size bronze statues of
US presidents. Of the forty-two on display, three are
featured with their dogs – George W. Bush, Gerald
Ford, and Warren G. Harding. Gerald Ford's golden
retriever, Liberty, was frequently photographed with
her master. It is rumoured that if Ford wanted to
tactfully end a conversation in the Oval Office he
would secretly signal to Liberty and she would
saunter up to the guest, wag her tail, and demand
attention. City of Presidents, 361 Main Street, Rapid
City, South Dakota 57701-2837, USA.

FIGURE 41: The Queen Mother
was every bit as devoted to her corgis
as the Queen has been.

FIGURE 42: This sculpture in Bachelor Park
in Windsor was created in 2015
by Lydia Karpinska.

ALL THE QUEEN'S CORGIS

It is perhaps fair to say that no international figure has been so linked with dogs as the Queen has with her corgis. This love affair has gone on for over eighty years; at age seven, Elizabeth was given a puppy called Dookie by her father, the future King George VI. Apparently she chose Dookie, as he had a longer tail than his littermates – 'So we can see whether he's pleased or not,' she said.[13] (Interestingly, it now illegal to dock the tails of Pembroke Welsh corgis unless for medical reasons.)

The late Queen Mother was also a great fan of these little dogs, and about halfway along the Mall is a beautiful and detailed bronze frieze by Paul Day featuring her sitting with two of them – Rush and Minnie. The Queen Mother is said to have instigated many of the routines that are still used around the royal dogs today. For example, she determined that each should have its own wicker basket to nap in and that these baskets should be placed on shelves to avoid draughts.

When the Queen turned eighteen, her mother and father gave her another corgi for her birthday whom she named Susan. Susan went on to be the common ancestor of all the Queen's corgis – fourteen generations in all.[14] The Queen seemed incredibly

fond of Susan, even taking her on honeymoon, hidden beneath a blanket in the royal coach. However, Susan was not always so popular with the Palace staff, especially after biting the Royal Clock Winder and a Grenadier Guard.

Dr Roger Mugford, an animal behaviourist who has worked as a pet trainer at the Palace, has provided some wonderful insights into the Queen's relationships with her dogs.[15] According to Mugford, Her Majesty always likes to feed the corgis herself and gets them to sit around in a circle and wait patiently while each is fed in turn, according to their age. What's more, each dog has a bespoke meal tailored to their particular dietary needs. Dr Mugford noted how the Queen seemed to relax and become at ease when talking about her dogs. Perhaps this is unsurprising – in a life ruled by protocol, pets must bring some much-needed fun. And of course dogs are great levellers: they do not care if we are resident at Buckingham Palace or the park bench.

Mugford recalls how the corgis tended to follow the Queen around the Palace in the manner of 'a moving carpet', as Princess Diana had jokingly observed, and that the Queen would often take them on her travels between royal residences. 'She personally used

FIGURE 43: One of the Queen's dorgis
(a cross between a corgi and a dachshund)
in Windsor.

FIGURE 44: Many of the dogs are shown scampering
around happily and they seemed to delight the small
children playing there when I visited. One little boy was
overheard saying: 'Why does that old lady have so many
dogs, Mummy?'

to drive the dogs along the highway linking Central London to Windsor Castle in a beat-up old General Motors Estate car,' Mugford confides, conjuring up a rather appealing image. 'I think she wore some disguise (such as one of her trademark silk scarves) while driving so that she wouldn't be recognised.'[15]

In common with many of us, the Queen appears to have derived therapeutic benefits from her dogs. Prince Philip has spoken of how she enjoys walking them, as it serves as a time for contemplation. And she is not above indulging her pets on special occasions: every Christmas, for example, she helps prepare stockings for them containing a cake, biscuit, and toy, the latter being strictly of the *non-squeaking* kind.[15]

To celebrate her ninetieth birthday, a lovely statue of the Queen with her dogs was installed in Windsor. Recently she has disclosed that she will not breed any more corgis as she wouldn't want to leave any behind when she dies. This seems poignant considering that the Welsh Pembroke corgi was for many years on the Kennel Club's list of vulnerable breeds.[16] However, recently this dip in popularity has been reversing and so it seems corgis will continue to charm royalty and commoners alike.

QUEEN VICTORIA'S PET OBSESSION

The current queen isn't our only animal-loving monarch. Queen Victoria (1837-1901) was also a big fan of pets.

The queen had what she herself described as a melancholy childhood with many strict rules and few chances to have fun with other children. Perhaps not surprisingly, she bonded closely with her childhood pet, a Cavalier King Charles spaniel called Dash. The fact that Dash was never far from her mind is illustrated by the story that even on her Coronation Day she took time out to give him a bath as soon as she got home.

The little dog also helped cement Victoria's relationship with the person who was to become her nearest and dearest – Albert. There is no doubt that Victoria was impressed with the handsome man with the 'large blue eyes and delightful expression', but the fact that he liked Dash probably didn't go amiss either. After their first meeting, she recorded in her diary that 'Albert played with and fussed over Dash.'[17]

Queen Victoria went on to have a great many pets in her lifetime (including over seventy dogs) and she was a staunch defender of animal rights. On her jubilees, for example, she had the authority to commute the sentences of prisoners throughout

THE QUEEN AND QUEEN MOTHER
The Queen Mother and her corgis reside on the Mall, London SW1A 2BJ.
Commemorating her ninetieth birthday, there is a statue of the Queen surrounded by her corgis and dorgis at Bachelor's Acre, Windsor SL4 1ER.

QUEEN VICTORIA AND ISLAY
The wishing well statue of Islay can be found outside The Queen Victoria Building, 455 George Street, Sydney NSW 2000, Australia. Also by this beautiful Romanesque Revival building you can see a statue of the Queen herself.
In Windsor Castle there is a large statue of Victoria with one of her collies at her side. Windsor Castle, Windsor SL4 1NJ.
And there is a statue of Bosco, one of the Queen's pugs, outside her bedroom window at Osborne House. York Avenue, East Cowes, Isle of Wight PO32 6JX. English Heritage.

FIGURE 45: Wishing well featuring a bronze sculpture of one of Queen Victoria's favourite dogs 'Islay', a Skye terrier. The statue, which was sculpted by Sydney artist Justin Robson, is said to be based on a drawing of the little dog begging, by the Queen herself. (For a tour of animal statues, including Islay, in Sydney, see this paper.[20])

the Empire, however she would always refuse to release those convicted of cruelty to animals.[18] She repeatedly lobbied parliament to introduce legislation to oversee the practice of vivisection, forcing the then prime minister, Disraeli, to call a royal commission on the subject. This resulted in the 1876 Cruelty to Animals Act that stated that the experiments must save or prolong human life and that the animals used must be anaesthetised and humanely killed.[19] This Act represented a huge step forward for animals, and although it has now been superseded by the Animals (Scientific Procedures) Act 1986, it has in many respects not changed appreciably.

Not content with this, Victoria also spoke out against the fashion at the time for the use of feathers, wings, and even whole birds in hats and boas. And she supported the Society for the Prevention of Cruelty to Animals (SPCA) by giving it royal status and thus giving rise to the RSPCA.

So more than any other British monarch, Victoria went out of her way to speak up for animals and bring about a softening of attitudes towards them, which, it

has been argued, occasionally verged on sentimentality.

While the Queen was interested in all animals, it was dogs that she seemed to love the most. She was particularly attached to her collies, Sharp and Noble, and was also a big fan of Skye terriers and Pomeranians. Poms, as they are often known, originate from medium-sized, sturdy spitz-type dogs used in sledge pulling. The Queen's preference for smaller examples meant that breeders supplied her with their very smallest Poms, and it was these dogs that became widespread and dominate today.[21] In January 1901, as the 81-year-old Queen lay dying, a last request was to have one of these beloved Poms, Turri, placed beside her on the bed.

JAMES CLERK WHO?
Unless you are a physicist or engineer, it is quite possible that you will have never heard of James Clerk Maxwell, which is a shame, as his contribution to physics is said to be right up there with Newton and Einstein. Maxwell (1831-79) set out the mathematical equations behind the electromagnetic theory of light and produced the world's first colour photograph.

FIGURE 46: James Clerk Maxwell with his colour wheel and Toby in Edinburgh.

His ideas paved the way for so many things we would find it hard to be without today – TV, radio, telecommunications, radar, even the Internet.

Maxwell grew up in Edinburgh and was an inquisitive lad. A letter from his parents describing their young son illustrates this: '"Show me how it doos" is never out of his mouth. He also investigates the hidden courses of streams and bell wires'.[22]

Aged ten, Maxwell was enrolled at the Edinburgh Academy. At first he was perceived as a bit of a loner with few friends and only average grades. In fact, Maxwell was given the nickname Dafty! But it wasn't long before he began to blossom academically.

After graduation, Maxwell moved south to Peterhouse College in Cambridge where he worked on a problem that had been perplexing scientists for a while – the nature of Saturn's rings. Maxwell decided that they must be composed of small particles orbiting the planet. (He was right – his predictions were confirmed over a century later by the Voyager space probe.) In 1860, he became a professor at King's College, London, where he would develop and publish his theories on electromagnetism. Not bad for a boy once named Dafty.

So where is the animal connection? Well, it seems that Maxwell was rather socially awkward and generally preferred the company of animals to people. We know that animals can help reduce social anxiety and that many people find them easier to bond with than their fellow humans, so perhaps Maxwell was tapping into this. It is said that he would often talk to his Irish terrier, Toby, outlining his latest theories to the little dog's non-discerning ear. He would also examine Toby's eyes with an ophthalmoscope in his efforts to understand colour blindness.

In 2008, a statue to Maxwell was unveiled in Edinburgh to mark the 175th anniversary of his birth. It shows him sitting on a chair with his 'colour wheel' and his dog Toby by his side. When the statue was being planned, Dr Duncan of The Royal Society of Edinburgh was keen to incorporate the dog to make the statue more accessible and broaden its appeal. James Rautio of Sonnet Software in the US who helped fund the project concurs, saying, 'Without the dog, from a child's point of view this is just some big statue of some dusty old guy that grown-ups insist is important.'[23] Much as I admire Maxwell, I'm inclined to agree.

JAMES CLERK MAXWELL AND TOBY
22-26 George Street, Edinburgh EH2 2PQ.

AN EDINBURGH DOG TRAIL

In addition to Toby, there are five other dog statues and memorials in Edinburgh, all happily within walking distance of each other. Greyfriars Bobby and his gravestone are on Candlemaker Row and in the nearby Kirkyard (see Chapter 5). Bum is tucked just inside the entrance to Princes Street Gardens – notice his shortened front leg (see Chapter 5). In Edinburgh Castle, there is a small cemetery of soldiers' dog graves. While there is no direct access to the cemetery, good views are afforded from above - look out for one of the older gravestones, dated 1881, that marks the resting place of Jess, a band mascot of the Black Watch 42nd Royal Highlanders. Finally, the famous writer, Sir Walter Scott, can be rightfully admired with his loyal Maida in the Scott Monument, E. Princes St Gardens (see Chapter 4).

References

1. Guegeun, N., and S. Ciccotii, D*omestic Dogs as Facilitators in Social Interaction: An Evaluation of Helping and Courtship Behaviors*, Anthrozoös 2008, 21(4), pp.339-49.
2. White House Pets (1953 - Present), The Presidential Pet Museum, http://www. presidentialpetmuseum.com/whitehousepets-1.
3. Maltzman, F., Lebovic, J.H., Saunders E.N., and E. Furth, *Unleashing Presidential Power: The Politics of Pets in the White House*, Political Science and Politics 45(3), pp.395-400.
4. Adamic, L., Burke, M., Herdagdelen, A., and D. Neumann, *Cat People, Dog People, Facebook Research*, 7 August 2016, https://research.fb.com/ cat-people-dog-people.
5. The Churchill Archive online – http://www. churchillarchive.com.
6. CHAR/28/27/65-66 Letter from WSC to Lady Randolph Churchill, 1981.
7. FDR, *"The Fala Speech"*, YouTube – https://www. youtube.com/watch?v=4gztvtSyTdY.
8. Roosevelt, E., 1992, *The Autobiography of Eleanor Roosevelt*, Da Capo Press, New York.
9. Wheeler, C., The Times, 4 February 2018, Paw job by Larry, No 10's mouser.
10. Chief Mouser to the Cabinet Office, Wikipedia.
11. Algeo, M., 2015, *Abe and Fido: Lincoln's Love of Animals and the Touching Story of his Favourite Companion*, Chicago Review Press, USA.
12. Coren, S., 2011, *Why Are Dogs so Frequently Called "Fido"?* Psychology Today blog, 12 October 2011, https://www. psychologytoday.com/blog/caninecorner/201110/why-are-dogs-so-frequently-calledfido.
13. *Corgi in Royal Favour.* The Cairns Post, 29 December 1952.
14. Gross, M.J., *Queen Elizabeth and Her Corgis: A Love Story*, Vanity Fair, August 2015.
15. Westenfeld, A., *Everything You've Ever Wanted to Know About Queen Elizabeth's Corgis*, Town and Country Magazine, 22 July 2015.
16. The Kennel Club, Save the Forgotten Dog Breeds Campaign, https://www.thekennelclub.org.uk/forgottenbreeds
17. The Cavalier Club, The Young Victoria, April 2009.
18. Border Wars, http://www.border-wars. com/2009/01/queen-victorias-border-collies.html.
19. Susan Hamilton, *On the Cruelty to Animals Act*, 15 August 1876, Branch Collective, http://www. branchcollective. org/?ps_articles=susan-hamiltonon-the-cruelty-to-animals-act-15-august-1876.
20. Kean, H., and A.L. Podberscek, *Looking at Some of the Animal Statues and Installations in Sydney*, www.isaz2018.com/assets/ isaz2018/Looking-at-some-of-the-animal-statues-in-Sydney.pdf.
21. The History of the Pomeranian, http://www. americanpomeranianclub.org/history.htm.
22. Johnson, K., 2002, *James Clerk Maxwell – The Great Unknown*, http://www-history.mcs.st-andrews.ac.uk/history/ Projects/ Johnson/index.html.
23. Rautio, J.C., *Maxwell's Home Preserved, His Statue Unveiled, but the Final Word Is from a Child*, IEEE Microwave Magazine, June 2009.

CHAPTER 4

Love me, love my pet

ARTY TYPES

In Chapter 3 we saw that the vast majority of US presidents shared their homes with at least one pet. Could the same be said of famous authors and artists?

Certainly many writers of the nineteenth and twentieth centuries owned and admired cats and dogs. Charles Dickens, Mark Twain, William Wordsworth, and Thomas Hardy were all fond of their pets, and Lewis Carroll created one of the most iconic feline images ever, through his Cheshire Cat in *Alice's Adventures in Wonderland*. What's more, both cats and dogs have long been the favoured subjects of painters – no surprise to those of us who admire the aesthetics of our pets.

Today, images of cats in particular are found on a huge variety of products and it is estimated that there are 1,000 shops in the US selling nothing but cat-themed items.

Interestingly, products featuring dogs seem not to sell as well.[1] One reason for this, merchandisers say, is that dog people are breed-oriented, so a poodle owner will probably not buy a mug with a German shepherd on it. A cat lover, on the other hand, will buy any and every kind of feline depiction. Hmm, guilty as charged.

In some cases the pets of artists and writers probably have provided much-needed companionship in what can be rather solitary professions. It's easy to imagine the dog curled at the feet of Tennyson or the cat lying languidly across the pages of Samuel Johnson's great work in progress, probably batting the writer's feather quill from time to time with his paws.

In others they were no doubt a direct source of inspiration. But whatever their role, many of these pets have gone on to be immortalised with statues and monuments. Let's take a look at these next.

The Story of Byron and Boatswain

With his moody good looks and eccentric aristocratic lifestyle, Byron (1788-1824) has long been credited as one of Britain's most accomplished romantic poets. He was also 'mad, bad, and dangerous to know', according to his lover, Lady Caroline Lamb. A rather irresistible description that only serves to make him sound more exciting.

In addition to his writing, Byron is also known for his love of animals and the fact that he shared his homes in England, Italy, Switzerland, and Greece with many of all shapes and sizes. The wonderfully bizarre nature of his menageries is illustrated in a letter by fellow poet Percy Shelley, who was a good friend of Byron:

> Lord B.'s establishment consists, besides servants, of ten horses, eight enormous dogs, three monkeys, five cats, an eagle, a crow, and a falcon; and all these, except the horses, walk about the house, which every now and then resounds with their unarbitrated quarrels, as if they were the masters of it. . . . I find that my enumeration of the animals in this Circean Palace was defective. . . . I have just met on the grand staircase five peacocks, two guinea hens, and an Egyptian crane.[2]

Byron seems to have been pretty determined not to be without animals at any stage of his life. While I was at University and missing my pets from home, I must admit to occasionally encouraging local cats into my room so I could get a bit of a cat fix. Well, Byron went several stages further. On attending Trinity College he circumvented University rules banning dogs by taking his tame bear along instead. It seems there was no mention in the college rulebook about bears not being allowed!

But of all the wondrous beasts sharing Byron's life, it is perhaps dogs that pulled on his heartstrings most, and of all the dogs he owned, his favourite seems to have been a Newfoundland called Boatswain.

Originally developed in the place of their name in Canada to assist the fishermen, the Newfoundlands' coat and webbed feet made them great swimmers able to cope with the extreme cold of Canadian waters. Striking and impressive in appearance, they were also known for their gentle natures and soon stories began circulating of the dogs performing heroic deeds. Because of this, in the eighteenth and nineteenth centuries Newfoundlands became highly prized and owning one was considered something of a status symbol. This surge in their popularity was

not lost on the perspicacious Newfoundlanders who soon began breeding dogs in Canada especially for export to Britain.[3] It is said that when the puppies arrived at ports around the UK they were greeted by crowds of excited people eager to purchase them.

Byron acquired Boatswain, who was probably a Newfoundland cross, when he was just fifteen years old. Perhaps one of the reasons the two bonded so well was that Boatswain brought an element of stability to Byron's days. The poet certainly lived a life of controversy. He is reported to have had many affairs and even intimate relations with his half-sister. As was the custom at this time, he would send locks of hair to his lovers. However, DNA analysis shows that most came not from the fine head of the poet himself but from a dog, quite possibly Boatswain! Perhaps there were so many amours that Byron simply didn't have sufficient hair to send to them all, whereas the shaggy Boatswain would have had it in abundance.

In 1808, aged just twenty, Byron took up residence at Newstead Abbey in Nottinghamshire. The Abbey has a large lake and the story goes that the poet would row into the middle with Boatswain and his other Newfoundland in the boat. He'd then leap

FIGURE 47 (opposite): Painting of Boatswain by Clifton Tomson. You may be forgiven for thinking that Boatswain does not look that typical of today's Newfoundlands. In his beautiful book on Byron[3], Geoffrey Bond notes that the exact origins of the Newfoundland are shrouded in mystery, with some claiming them to be the descendants of mastiff-like dogs and others pointing to an Eskimo dog/husky ancestor. While early Newfoundlands showed considerable diversity in size and shape, they all seemed to have possessed a suitably noble mien.

'Newfoundland dogs are good to save children from drowning, but you must have a pond of water handy and a child, or else there will be no profit in boarding a Newfoundland.'

Josh Billings

overboard and get the dogs to ferry him back to shore. Interestingly, amongst the many Victorian tales of Newfoundlands saving people from drowning, there are some less flattering reports of dogs so obsessed with rescuing that they would grab hold of people enjoying a pleasant dip and determinedly drag them ashore against their will![3]

Sadly, Byron's time with his much-loved dog was not to last long. Less than a year after moving to Newstead, Boatswain contracted rabies. It was thought he must have been bitten by another dog when he was following the post boy to the nearby village of Mansfield. In the early nineteenth century, rabies was common throughout England and a cause of understandable fear. So much so, in fact, that the government offered a reward of up to five shillings for each rabid dog killed.[4]

Distraught, Byron remained with the terribly ill Boatswain, nursing him and putting himself at considerable risk in doing so. Despite all his efforts, the dog could not be saved. In a letter Byron wrote to his friend and fellow writer Francis Hodgson, he said, 'Boatswain is dead! He expired in a state of madness on the 18th suffering much yet retaining all the gentleness of his nature to the last, never attempting to do the least injury to those near him.'[5]

After the death, and despite being much in debt, Byron commissioned a marble monument for his Boatswain at Newstead on the site of the former Abbey's ruins.

The epitaph, which has become one of Byron's best-known works, and its introduction, written by his friend John Cam Hobhouse (in italics), reads as follows:[6]

Near this Spot
are deposited the Remains of one
who possessed Beauty without Vanity,

Strength without Insolence,
Courage without Ferocity,
and all the virtues of Man without his Vices.

This praise, which would be unmeaning Flattery
if inscribed over human Ashes,
is but a just tribute to the Memory of
Boatswain, a Dog
who was born in Newfoundland May 1803
and died at Newstead Nov. 18th, 1808

When some proud Son of Man returns to Earth,
Unknown to Glory, but upheld by Birth,
The sculptor's art exhausts the pomp of woe,
And storied urns record who rests below.
When all is done, upon the Tomb is seen,
Not what he was, but what he should have been.
But the poor Dog, in life the firmest friend,
The first to welcome, foremost to defend,
Whose honest heart is still his Master's own,
Who labours, fights, lives, breathes for him alone,
Unhonoured falls, unnoticed all his worth,
Denied in heaven the Soul he held on earth –
While man, vain insect! hopes to be forgiven,
And claims himself a sole exclusive heaven.

Oh man! thou feeble tenant of an hour,
Debased by slavery, or corrupt by power –
Who knows thee well, must quit thee with disgust,
Degraded mass of animated dust!
Thy love is lust, thy friendship all a cheat,
Thy tongue hypocrisy, thy heart deceit!
By nature vile, ennobled but by name,
Each kindred brute might bid thee blush for shame.
Ye, who behold perchance this simple urn,
Pass on – it honours none you wish to mourn.
To mark a friend's remains these stones arise;
I never knew but one – and here he lies.

Dr Johnson and His 'Very Fine Cat'

Samuel Johnson (1709-84) may not have had the brooding looks of Byron, but he is counted as one of Britain's finest literary figures. He was a prolific writer who produced essays, biographies, poetry, and critiques. But probably his most famous work was his *Dictionary of the English Language*, a mammoth undertaking that took over eight years (although, the fact that he rarely got up before midday may have partly explained why it took so long). Completed in 1755, it contains quite a few amusing definitions such as:

> Dull: Not exhilarating [*sic*]; not delightful; as, to make dictionaries is dull work
> Mouth-friend: Someone who pretends to be your friend

The dictionary was not replaced for an incredible 150 years, when the *Oxford English Dictionary* was published. As if these accolades weren't enough, according to the *Oxford Book of Quotations*, Johnson is also the most quoted Englishman after Shakespeare.

Born in Lichfield, Staffordshire, to a bookseller, poor Johnson's life was certainly not without adversity. When he was born he was baptised immediately, as it

wasn't thought he'd survive. As a baby he had problems with his sight and hearing, and catching tuberculosis at the age of two seems to have left him with facial scarring. Clearly an intelligent boy, he went to study at Oxford University, but had to leave after a year since his parents could no longer afford the fees. Without a degree, Johnson found it difficult to fulfil his dream of becoming a teacher. He was also hampered by what were considered strange mannerisms or tics. These are now thought to be the symptoms of Tourette's, but at the time they led some to conclude that Johnson was intellectually inferior. Scholars also believe he suffered various bouts of depression and may have contemplated suicide. With all this to cope with, perhaps it is no wonder that one of Johnson's quotes states that 'It is by affliction chiefly that the heart of man is purified.'

And indeed, Johnson seems to have been very pure of heart, being a sociable and highly compassionate man. He disapproved of slavery and bequeathed his estate to a former slave from Jamaica after he and his family came to work for him. He helped others who were stricken down by poverty and of course he was a cat lover, having at least two cats, Hodge and Lily. In his biography of Johnson, his good friend, the lawyer Boswell, who clearly was not a cat fan, states,

FIGURE 48 (opposite): Lexi at Boatswain's tomb. The large, ornate urn was a common decoration from the late 1700's and is thought to symbolise the liberation of the soul. Byron was active in the classical debate raging at the time as to whether animals had souls.

The poet had wished to be buried with his favourite dog, a wish that was sadly denied by the new owners of the Abbey. (He is interred instead at the Church of St Mary Magdalene nearby.)[7] His request seems to resonate increasingly with pet owners today, and in the last decade planning permission has been granted in the UK for more and more joint animal/human cemeteries.

BYRON AND BOATSWAIN
Newstead Abbey Historic House and Park, Ravenshead, Nottinghamshire NG15 8NA. Admission fee applies.
In addition to the memorial at Newstead, there is also a statue of Byron, looking magnificent in his thoughtfulness with Boatswain in London. Unfortunately, this beautiful monument is marooned in a sea of traffic meaning you will need to have something of a death wish to view it up close. Behind Aplsey House on a traffic island in Park Lane, off Hyde Park, London W1.

I never shall forget the indulgence with which he treated Hodge, his cat: for whom he himself used to go out and buy oysters, lest the servants having that trouble should take a dislike to the poor creature. I am, unluckily, one of those who have an antipathy to a cat, so that I am uneasy when in the room with one; and I own, I frequently suffered a good deal from the presence of this same Hodge. I recollect him one day scrambling up Dr Johnson's breast, apparently with much satisfaction, while my friend smiling and half-whistling, rubbed down his back, and pulled him by the tail; and when I observed he was a fine cat, saying, 'Why yes, Sir, but I have had cats whom I liked better than this;' and then as if perceiving Hodge to be out of countenance, adding, 'but he is a very fine cat, a very fine cat indeed.'[8]

Boswell also noted how Johnson cared for Hodge when the cat was nearing his end by going out to buy valerian, presumably to bring about drowsiness and ease the poor cat's suffering.

Were Dr Johnson's slightly indulgent views on cats representative of many at the time? Seemingly not. Cats and kittens do occasionally feature in art from the eighteenth and early nineteenth century, but much less frequently than dogs.[9] Their appeal broadened among the wealthy in the Victorian era, partly thanks to the interest in Egyptology and the reverence ancient Egyptians held for their felines, and partly as a result of Queen Victoria, who, while mostly known for her love of dogs, also showed an interest in cats. However, among the middle and poorer classes, they were still chiefly seen as rodent catchers.

The bronze statue of Hodge by Jon Bickley was unveiled in 1997 by Lord Mayor of London, Sir Roger Cook, in a courtyard outside Johnson's house, which is now a museum dedicated to the writer. Hodge is shown sitting on top of Johnson's dictionary, next to some empty oyster shells. The monument is inscribed with the words 'a very fine cat indeed'. It is interesting that the City of London chose to commemorate Johnson through his cat rather than by a statue of himself or some other kind of memorial. (See reference for a discussion on this.[10])

Bickley modelled the statue on his own cat and ensured that Hodge sits at about waist height, 'just right,' so he said, 'for adults to put their arm around.'[11] In the short time I was there taking photographs I never witnessed anyone hug Hodge, but I did watch three different groups of people come by specifically to see him and use their mobile phones to listen to his story, for Hodge is one of London's talking statues – monuments that come to life with the voice of a celebrity telling their story.

Just before taking my leave, and after looking around to check no one was looking, I went up to Hodge to say goodbye – and, oh, give him a quick hug.

A Painter and His Pug: William Hogarth

The website of the West London information agency, ChiswickW4, playfully suggests that while Chiswick may not have a Trump Towers as in New York, it is almost certainly the only place in Britain to have a statue to Trump.[12] In this case, Trump the pug!

Unveiled by The William Hogarth Trust on 10 November 2001 to coincide with the Chiswick painter's birthday, the statue features the famous

HODGE
17 Gough Square, London EC4A 3DE, opposite the
Samuel Johnson museum.

FIGURE 49: The inscription on the monument reads:
Hodge, 'a very fine cat indeed' belonging to
Samuel Johnson (1709 -1784) of Gough Square.
'Sir, when a man is tired of London he is tired of life: for
there is in London all that life can afford.'
'The chief glory of every people arises
from its authors.'

artist with his pet pug, who shares the president's name. At first the statue was planned without the pug, but the Trust felt the addition of the dog would help reflect Hogarth's kindness and humanity. Every year since, on Hogarth's birthday, a wreath of flowers has been placed on the statue.

Hogarth (1697-1764) is thought to be the first English artist to attract international attention. As well as being a renowned painter, engraver, and cartoonist, he was also someone who wore his heart very much on his painter's smock sleeve and was an active campaigner against injustice. Perhaps this was because his father fell on hard times during Hogarth's childhood and ended up in debtor's prison.

Hogarth was also a great satirist whose work often featured the seamier side of London life. Two of his best-known engravings, *Gin Lane* and *Beer Street*, aimed to show the evils of consuming cheap gin compared to the merits of drinking beer! These engravings helped bring in the Gin Act of 1751 that reduced the number of shops selling the spirit cheaply.

In the same year, Hogarth produced *The Four Stages of Cruelty* in which he depicts the bad treatment of animals, something he saw all around him and that troubled him deeply. He was also fond of children, and although he and his wife never had their own, they did foster some from the local Foundling Hospital. Perhaps Hogarth's most famous work is his self-portrait with his pug, which inspired the Chiswick monument.

Looking at the statue of Trump, you are likely to be struck by how different he looks to the pugs of today.

He is considerably longer in the legs and his face is not as flattened. Pugs are believed to have descended from Chinese happa dogs and were brought from that country to Europe some 400-500 years ago when countries like the Netherlands and Portugal were trading in Asia. Once in Europe they were developed into their current form via selective breeding – where individual dogs with desired traits are mated.[13] In 1873, when the UK Kennel Club was founded, it produced standards for each dog breed based on the work of the early breeders. This was the template for those breeding dogs to aspire to and the standard they would be judged against at shows. Unfortunately, characteristics that the Victorians and later generations had found desirable were not always in the animal's best interest and could lead to serious health problems.

To help correct this, the Kennel Club began revising the standards and in 2009 launched the online health tool, Breed Watch.[14] This aims to provide information on breed-specific health concerns, which, in the case of the pug includes difficulty breathing and excessively prominent eyes. Judges at dog shows are now able to report on these problems and breeders should no longer select dogs for mating that have such exaggerated traits.

You can see the statue of Hogarth and Trump in Chiswick; endearingly, The William Hogarth Trust also commissioned a copy of Trump for the playground of The William Hogarth School. So now the children have their very own pug to play with.[15]

WALTER SCOTT (1771-1832) AND HIS LOVE FOR DOGS
Maida, Camp, Spice, Nimrod, Ginger, and Triton were all dogs owned and beloved by Sir Walter Scott (1771-1832). Scott was a hugely successful poet and the author of classics such as *Ivanhoe* and *Rob Roy*.

HOGARTH AND TRUMP
147 Chiswick High Road, Chiswick, London W4 2DT.
You can view the portrait at Tate Britain, London
SW1P 4RG (Display room 1730).

FIGURE 50: Hogarth in painting pose with Trump. It is interesting that Trump is not looking up devotedly at his owner, as are many of the dogs in older sculptures. (see figs 51-54 for example). Perhaps this reflects the modernity of the piece, although having known several excellent pugs I can affirm that they only looked at me devotedly when I was eating!

His stories, which were packed with romance and chivalry, are thought by many to be the world's first historical novels and his Waverley books provided the name for Edinburgh's Waverley railway station.

Certainly, there can be little doubt that Scott loved his dogs and many portraits of the writer include the animals sitting or lying at his feet. One of his favourites was Camp, a bull terrier that he acquired at the time of his marriage in 1797. In a description of Camp, he describes the terrier thus:

> He was of great strength and very handsome, extremely sagacious faithful and affectionate to the human species and possessed of a great turn for gaiety and drollery. Although he was never taught any tricks he learned some of his own accord and understood whatever was said to him as well as any creature I ever saw. His great fault was an excessive ferocity towards his own species which sometimes brought his Master and himself into dangerous scrapes.[16]

When Camp died, Scott buried him in his garden opposite the window where he would sit writing. He was clearly much affected by the loss and states in a letter, 'I was rather more grieved than philosophy admits of & he has made a sort of blank which nothing will fill up for a long while.'

Sentiments that will no doubt strike a chord with many pet owners today. In fact, Scott seems to have pondered a good deal over the death of his dogs and is also quoted as saying,

> I have sometimes thought of the final cause of dogs having such short lives and I am quite satisfied it is in compassion to the human race; for if we suffer so much in losing a dog after an acquaintance of ten or twelve years, what would it be if they were to live double that time?

After Scott himself died, a competition was held to design a monument in Edinburgh to his memory. Enter joiner and carpenter George Meikle Kemp. Son of a poor shepherd, Kemp had a burning passion for architecture, but no qualifications. Fearing this might count against him, he submitted his design under the pseudonym John Morvo, a sixteenth-century mason who worked on Melrose Abbey. In actual fact his true identity was accidentally discovered by the judges, but it didn't matter. Subject to a few amendments, Kemp's design was selected and he was given the contract.

The structure Kemp designed is reported to be the world's largest monument to a writer. Within the columns of this 200ft-high, gothic tower is a marble statue of the man himself, designed by John Steele. The statue shows Scott sitting with quill pen in hand, while his deerhound, Maida, gazes up at him. Maida was named after a Napoleonic battle and he (for Maida was a male dog) also appears in a statue guarding the entrance to Scott's home – Abbotsford.

If you feel reasonably fit and don't suffer from vertigo, it is well worth climbing the narrow, spiral staircase to the top of the Scott Monument. It is nearly 300 steps in all, but there are opportunities to rest on the way and you can admire some amazing views while you get your breath back. There are sixty-eight mini statues on the monument, each representing a

THE SCOTT MONUMENT
The Scott Monument is lit up every night. It can be found at E. Princes Street Gardens, Edinburgh EH2 2EJ.

'You think dogs will not be in heaven? I tell you, they will be there long before any of us.'

Robert Louis Stevenson

FIGURE 51: Walter Scott and Maida (Edinburgh). Scott described Maida as 6ft long and iron strong.

FIGURE 52 (opposite): Tennyson and his dog outside the beautiful Lincoln Cathedral.

character from one of Scott's books, and if you look closely you may spot the farmer Dandie Dinmont from the novel *Guy Mannering*. Dinmont has a little dog at his feet that went on to become a recognised breed – the Dandie Dinmont terrier.[17]

The sight of this enormous and beautiful monument, with all its intricate miniature sculptures, is something to behold, but sadly its story is not without tragedy. A few months before it was due to be inaugurated, Kemp was walking along the Union Canal to his home in Morningside. It seems he must have lost his way in the fog that had descended and he fell into the water and drowned.

Kemp is buried in St Cuthberts churchyard in a grave facing the monument he designed.

MORE WRITERS AND THEIR DOGS

Tennyson The poet Lord Tennyson (1809-92) is remembered in Lincoln, the place of his birth, with a statue in the grounds of Lincoln Cathedral. This impressive monument is the work of George Frederick Watts, a friend of Tennyson's, who began the sculpture a year after the poet's death, when he himself was in his eighties. Sadly, Watts never got to see his work unveiled, as he died a year before it was erected. The statue also shows Tennyson's dog, a wolfhound known as Karenina. There is a dastardly rumour that Karenina was only added to stop the

statue toppling over. However, I prefer to think that she, and the flower in the writer's hand, were added to celebrate Tennyson's love of nature and animals. Lincoln Cathedral, Lincoln LN2.

Robert Louis Stevenson penned such classics as *Treasure Island* and *Dr Jekyll and Mr Hyde*. His endearing statue may be viewed in a village just outside Edinburgh – Colinton Parish Church, Dell Road, Colinton, Edinburgh EH13 0JR.

Burns Robert Burns (1759-96) died aged just thirty-seven, but in his short lifetime he produced many celebrated literary works, including the incomparable New Year's favourite: 'Auld Lang Syne'. Among Burns' greatest loves was his border collie, Luath (a name meaning swift or fleet in Gaelic). The two were said to be inseparable and there is a suggestion that Burns met his future wife, Jean Armour, after she chased the dog away from playing with some washing she'd put out to dry. Statues of Burns with his faithful dog, Luath, can be found in various countries including: Sturt Street, Ballarat, Victoria and Centenary Place, Brisbane, Australia; Winthrop Square and The Fenway in Boston, Massachusetts; and Greyfriars Church, Dumfries, Scotland.

James Herriot The much-loved Yorkshire vet and writer, whose real name was Alf Wight, is celebrated in a statue where he is shown holding a little dog. The World of James Herriot, 23 Kirkgate, Thirsk YO7 1PL.

FIGURE 53 (above): Robert Louis Stevenson
and Cuillin in Edinburgh.

FIGURE 54 (right): Robbie Burns
and his faithful Luath (Ballarat, Australia)

REFERENCES
 1. Dickinson, E., *All About/Cat Supplies; Billions for Food, and Knicknacks to Boot*, 22 July 1990.
 2. Moore, T., *Letters and Journals of Lord Byron*, London, 1830, p.612.
 3. Bondeson, J., 2011, *Amazing Dogs: A Cabinet of Canine Curiosities,* Cornell University Press, New York.
 4. Rendell, M., *Rabies in the Eighteenth Century* – http://mikerendell.com/rabies-in-the-eighteenthcentury.
 5. Elze, K.F., 1872, *Lord Byron, a Biography,* John Murray, London.
 6. Wikipedia, *Epitaph to a Dog*, https://en.wikipedia.org/wiki/Epitaph_to_a_Dog.
 7. Treneman A., 2016, *Finding the Plot: One Hundred Graves to Visit before You Die*, Biteback Publishing, London.
 8. Boswell J., 1791, *Life of Samuel Johnson*, Penguin Classic, London.
 9. Kean., H., 1998, *Animal Rights: Political and Social Change in Britain since 1800*, Reaktion Books, UK.
10. Kean., H. *Traces and Representations: Animal Pasts in London's Present,* The London Journal, 36(1).
11. Roberts, P., Purr 'n' Fur website, Hodge the cat.
12. *'Pugnacious' Character Unmoved by Birthday Celebration for Owner,* Chiswick W4.com, http://www.chiswickw4.com/default.as?
        section=info&page=hogarthbirthday004trump.htm.
13. *Pugs Have Changed a Bunch,* Retrieverman, https://retrieverman.net/2012/04/22/pugs-havechanged-a-bunch.
14. The Kennel Club, Breed Watch, http://www. thekennelclub.org.uk/services/public/breed/watch/Default.aspx.
15. William Hogarth Trust, *Pug Statue for Hogarth School,* https://williamhogarthtrust.org.uk/?page_id=114.
16. *Camp: Scott's Favourite Dog*, Walter Scott Library digital archive, Edinburgh University. http://www.walterscott.lib.ed.ac.uk/
        portraits/miscellaneous/camp.html.
17. Edinburgh City of Literature, *Sir Walter Scott – Father of the Dandie Dinmont?* http://www.cityofliterature.com/
        sir-walter-scottfather-dandie-dinmont.

CHAPTER 5

Bravery and service

ALWAYS ON DUTY

WALL PAINTINGS SHOW THAT animals such as dogs have played a part in human wars from ancient times. Greeks, Persians, Egyptians, Britons, and Romans all employed dogs, sometimes as sentries, but also in active fighting.[1] Ancient Rome used giant Molossian hounds equipped with coats of mail and spiked collars in their military conflicts (see Chapter 1). Fast forward to the Middle Ages, and other large breeds like mastiffs were used by the Spanish against the Native Americans and by Elizabeth I against the Irish. Napoleon too used dogs in his many campaigns and is said to have been moved by their loyalty.

An early official use of dogs for military purposes in the US was during the American Civil War. Here they would carry messages and act as guards and mascots. One such canine was the indomitable Sallie Ann Jarrett.

SALLIE THE BULLET-CHASING STAFFIE

Sallie Ann was the mascot for the 11th Pennsylvania Volunteer Infantry. From the one picture that remains of her, it seems she was a Staffordshire bull terrier or similar breed. Her name is said to have been derived from that of the colonel commanding the regiment – Colonel P. Jarrett – and a 'certain young lady in a nearby town' whom the men much admired.[2]

Sallie first went into combat at Cedar Mountain. Far from panicking under fire, she amused those around her by repeatedly trying to attack enemy bullets as they zipped into the ground! Sallie went on to accompany her regiment during many campaigns. She is said to have always been at the head of the march, rushing forward and barking furiously. On one sortie she was shot in the neck, the bullet going too deep to be removed. Did that slow Sallie down? Well, not for long – just a few days later she was back in action.[3]

During July 1863, on the first day of fighting at Gettysburg, Sallie was separated from the rest of her regiment during their retreat and it was feared that she must have been killed. Her location had been overtaken by the Confederate army and she would have been unable to pass through their lines to reunite with her regiment. In fact, Sallie had made her way to the 11th Pennsylvania's previous location on Oak Ridge. Here a member of her brigade found her three days later, keeping watch over the dead and wounded soldiers from their regiment.[3]

But Sallie was not to survive the war. Sadly, just a few months before its end she was killed by an enemy bullet to the head. Even though the soldiers with her were under heavy fire, they still laid down their arms to bury her.[4]

In 1890, the veterans of the 11th erected a monument at Gettysburg to all those who had fallen. The monument features a granite pedestal upon which stands the imposing figure of a skirmisher. And at the foot of the monument is a life-size bronze statue of Sallie.

ANIMALS IN WWI AND WWII

With the arrival of modern weaponry, animals began to take on less confrontational roles, but their use continued to be as important as ever. According to

the Imperial War Museum, 16 million animals were employed over the course of WWI.[5] Some, like horses and camels, mostly helped in transporting food, medical supplies, ammunition, and the wounded. Others, such as dogs and carrier pigeons, played vital roles in communication. Cats were employed as ratters, and of course both cats and dogs, just as in civilian life, would have boosted morale. Let's take a closer look at their roles during both World Wars.

Mogs of War

Enter the word 'cat' into the search box in the collections area of the Imperial War Museum website and you will be in for a treat. Up will pop pictures of smiling Polish sailors holding squirming kittens, furry faces peeping out from the ends of giant gun barrels, or cats sitting pretty on seaplane propellers. Cats, as we know, have always been fabulously photogenic.

During WWI, many regiments had cats with them at the western front. Unsurprisingly, rats and mice were a problem in the trenches and so a good ratter was pretty essential. Rat catchers were also much valued on Royal Navy and Merchant ships, where rodents could completely destroy food sources. Hence many of these ships had a moggie (or several) on board.

As with dogs, cats were also mascots and fun to have around. Taking time out to watch cats playing must have been a welcome diversion from the trials of war and in some cases a reminder of cats the servicemen

had at home. For those of a superstitious inclination, they were also good luck charms.

Something I have wondered about is how cats dealt with all the noise and commotion. My old cat, for example, would tear upstairs and disappear under the bed if I so much as opened a can of cola. Gilbert Adshead of *HMS Lord Nelson* recalls how the ship's cats coped (or not):

> We had a black and a tabby cat. Now, the strange thing about the black cat was, gunfire never worried him a bit. He'd walk about on the top of a 12 inch turret when the 12 inch gun was firing. . . . His fur would stand right, completely up on end. He'd just look round and see what was happening, and never move. The tabby cat was terror-stricken. It was a long time before we found where he used to hide.[7]

One very famous ratter who can truly be said to have gone above and beyond was Simon. His story is heart-warming, but, as is often the case, rather bittersweet. It began in March 1948 when the Royal Navy's *HMS Amethyst* called at the dockyard on Stonecutters Island in Hong Kong for supplies. Noticing a stray cat looking somewhat bedraggled, a young sailor decided to smuggle him aboard. It wasn't long before the ship's captain became aware of the feline stowaway, but luckily he was a cat lover and happy for Simon to stay – at least if he earned

SALLIE

Gettysburg National Military Park, 1195 Baltimore Pike, Gettysburg, Pennsylvania 17325, USA.

'Perhaps it was the spirit of the time and place that affected me. . . yet, here I was stirred, profoundly stirred, stirred to tears. And by what? By the grief of one dog. . . '[6]

Napoleon on seeing a dog whining and licking the hand of his dead soldier companion on an Italian battlefield.

FIGURE 55 (opposite): Sallie the staffie taking some well-earned rest at the foot of the Gettysburg memorial.

his stripes keeping the rats down. Something Simon proved very good at.[7]

In the spring of 1949, the *Amethyst* received orders to travel up the Yangtze River to relieve the ship *HMS Consort,* which was guarding the British Embassy in Nanking. China was in the midst of a communist revolution and the embassy staff would have to be evacuated should Mao Zedong's forces take control of the town. Unfortunately, barely 100 miles up the river, the *Amethyst* came under heavy shelling by the communist rebels and while trying to escape the fire, she ran aground on a sandbar. The attack led to twenty-five crew members being killed, including the captain, with many more injured. The ship remained stuck for 100 days before finally escaping back to the open sea. During the three months the ship was trapped, Simon, who had also been injured, continued to rid the ship of rats. This was vital since in the humid conditions rodent numbers were increasing rapidly and threatening the diminishing food stores.

As the ship sailed back to the safety of Hong Kong, news of their ordeal spread and the crew, including Simon and the ship's dog Peggy, were hailed as heroes. The Armed Forces Mascot Club, which was part of the People's Dispensary for Sick Animals (PDSA), recommended that Simon be awarded their Dickin medal (also known as the Animals' Victoria Cross).

Simon is the only feline recipient of this award. Sadly, however, he never got to receive it. The little cat died while still in quarantine in Surrey. He had contracted enteritis and it was thought that the injuries he'd sustained on the ship had weakened his heart.

Simon is buried in Ilford animal cemetery in Essex along with twelve other Dickin award recipients. Founded in the 1920s by the PDSA, this cemetery has the graves of many military animals. It is also a resting place for thousands of pets killed on official

advice at the start of WWII. There is no memorial recognising them here,[8] however one has recently been unveiled at the Old Blue Cross pet cemetery (see figure 58). In the 1960s, Ilford cemetery was closed, but in 2007, thanks to support from the National Lottery, it reopened and now members of the public can visit Simon's grave along with the many other memorials.

Present at the re-opening ceremony was Lt Commander Hett, who had been an officer aboard *HMS Amethyst* with Simon and who had been in charge of replying to Simon's considerable fan mail. When Hett was asked if he considered that a cat could be described as brave, he replied, 'Is it right to call an animal a hero? I think so, yes. To continue doing everything required of you under fire, to continue giving comfort and succour to your comrades, yes I think you could properly call that bravery.'[9]

'To arms, to arms, you dogs of Britain!'[10]

While cats certainly played their part, it is dogs who featured most in wartime efforts. In their fascinating book, the Campbells suggest that up to 20,000 British dogs were trained for duties during WWI, while Germany employed around 30,000.[11]

Some of the British dogs were family pets with the rest being rescue or police dogs. They included a wide range of breeds such as Dobermans, German shepherds (referred to at the time by the non-Teutonic name of Alsatians), Labradors, bloodhounds, collies, terriers, and Heinz 57 mongrels.[11]

It was the Germans who in 1884 set up what seems to be the first-ever military dog training school. Their methods, as with many modern methods, encouraged training by reward and went on to be used in military schools the world over. In 1911, Britain would establish its own training centre run by Lt Col Richardson in Woking, Surrey.[11]

There were a myriad ways in which dogs assisted in the war. Guard and patrol dogs would keep lookout at important military installations including railways, bridges, and ammunition stores. Sentinel dogs lay atop trenches, silently watching. They would alert to the approach of an enemy with a low growl or, as a story in the *Dundee Evening Telegraph* from 1916 reports, a 'pricking of the ears and the attitude of expectancy'.[12]

Scouting dogs had to be similarly quiet and disciplined. These dogs patrolled the area just ahead of their handlers and it is believed they could detect an enemy scent up to 1,000 yards away.[12] Like sentinel dogs, they would signal enemy encroachment with a stiffening of their body, or, if their handler had nodded off, licking them awake.

Dogs were also employed in laying telegraph wires from reels mounted on their backs and relaying messages. Messenger dogs were particularly useful when the phones went down, which seems to be not infrequently. They were faster than humans, especially over the tough terrain where they would have to negotiate shell holes, barbed wire, and even chemical gas, and they posed less of a target to enemy fire. Messages would be placed in small metal canisters attached to the collar, and the dogs, who had two different masters, one at each base, would diligently relay the messages between them.[13]

Often forgotten about are the little cigarette dogs. (See references for a wonderful video clip.)[14] These YMCA-sponsored bulldogs wore saddlebags stuffed with cigarettes that they took to the soldiers at the frontline.

Perhaps most poignant, though, were the dogs employed by the Red Cross. These casualty or 'mercy dogs', which were often bloodhounds, collies or Airedales, carried packs of medical supplies and would seek out the wounded on battlefields. Soldiers who were capable could use the supplies, while those who were fatally injured were at least comforted by the presence of the dog as they lay dying.[15]

At the beginning of WWII, there was a perception that dogs wouldn't have as big a role as they had in WWI, and pleas to the War Office by Lt Col Richardson to allow him to train more canines and 'collect and organise the dog power of this country' fell on deaf ears.[16] What's more, The National Veterinary Medical Association was actually advising pet owners that the kindest thing they could do was to have their pets put to sleep. They noted that pets would not be allowed in air-raid shelters, nor would they be provided with gas masks. They would, however, likely be scared out of their wits by the bombing that might soon take place and they would certainly be a drain on Britain's much-needed food rations. This advice was taken to heart by many, and in her book,

FIGURE 56 (opposite): Cats sit anywhere, including the propeller shafts of seaplanes.

FIGURE 57: Soldier inserting a note into the adapted collar of a messenger dog at the front during WW1.

Hilda Kean writes that 400,000 pets were killed in the first four days of the war, that is 26 per cent of cats and dogs in London.[8] Government, veterinary associations, and animal charities were opposed to this action, and later in the war many people came to regret their decision.[8]

As the war progressed, the need to free up men by using dogs to guard and patrol sensitive areas such as airfields was becoming increasingly apparent. And when the Blitz began in 1940, there was an obvious use for dogs helping casualties trapped in the rubble. In May 1941, those owners who had kept their dogs were targeted by advertisements in the press and on the wireless.[16]

'To British Dog Owners,' said the ads. 'Your country needs dogs for defence. Alsatians, Collies and other large breeds. Here is your great opportunity to actively help win the war – will you loan one?'[17]

Within a few weeks, 7,000 dogs were offered up. Some of these were used to help sniff out mines. Others, during the D-Day landings, were parachuted into France with their masters. Unfortunately, few of those that went to war returned. Of those that did, some lucky ones were reunited with their owners and a number were awarded Dickin medals. These awards continue to be given out today and of the sixty-eight currently awarded, thirty-one have been presented to dogs; four to horses; one to the cat, Simon; and thirty-two to pigeons.[18] One WWII recipient, an Air Raid Precautions (ARP) dog called Rex, was given his award with this commendation:

For outstanding good work in the location of casualties in burning buildings. Undaunted by smouldering debris, thick smoke, intense

heat and jets of water from fire hoses, this dog displayed uncanny intelligence and outstanding determination in his efforts to follow up any scent which led him to a trapped casualty.[9]

Many people have long believed that actions such as these deserve to be commemorated, and on 10 November 2004 (the ninetieth anniversary of the start of WWI) they finally were when the Princess Royal unveiled the Animals in War Memorial in Park Lane. Created from Portland stone, engraved with animal silhouettes and featuring two mules, a dog, and a horse cast in bronze, the memorial's size and imagery certainly stirs emotions. It bears two inscriptions that read,

'This monument is dedicated to all the animals that served and died alongside British and Allied forces in wars and campaigns throughout time.'
'They had no choice.'

The three parts of the memorial each have a special symbolism. The two heavily laden mules approaching the wall on the lower level represent the struggle through the war experience. On the upper level, beyond the wall, a dog looks back regretfully at his comrades and a huge and powerful horse seems to be soldiering on, unbeaten.

When I visited this memorial in May 2017, it was surrounded by a display of spring flowers. I stood with a group of fellow sightseers reading the inscriptions and for a while the noise of the cars and buses on Park Lane faded as we were silently absorbed by our thoughts. However, the memorial is not without its detractors. George Monbiot (quoted in H. Kean's

FIGURE 58: In August 2019, Clare (author of *Bonzo's War*[16]) and Christy Campbell unveiled a lovely plaque in the Old Blue Cross Pet Cemetery. Dedicated to the 2.9 million pets put to sleep under official advice at the start of WW2, it was created after Nicola White, a mudlark, found a dog tag entitled Bonzo Tabner by the Thames. Tracing his now very elderly owners, Nicola found that poor Bonzo had been one of those to suffer this sad fate.

paper[19]) maintains that emphasis given to animals' suffering in war highlights a failure to acknowledge human suffering and has led to a 'Disneyfication' of warfare.

MODERN MILITARY CONFLICTS

After WWII, dogs have continued to feature in our military campaigns. Some of their roles, such as guarding and patrolling, remain little changed since WWI, but now there are new roles that reflect the increasingly technical nature of battle. In places such as Afghanistan and Iraq, dogs are often used in the detection of explosives and drugs. Thankfully, they now have more protection and are kitted out with high-tech flak jackets.[20]

Legislation has been passed in many countries that protects the welfare of working dogs, and retired military dogs can now be adopted by their handler's families or, after specialist training, into homes on civvy street. This is a far cry from what happened after the war in Vietnam. Around 5,000 American dogs served in the Vietnam War mostly to guard gun towers and bunkers, and they were highly successful in alerting the Americans to Viet Cong intruders.[2.] Despite a public outcry, at the end of the war many of these dogs were simply euthanised or left behind. A memorial in Riverside, California features a number of engraved tiles bearing inscriptions to individual

dogs who served in Korea and Vietnam. One such tile is inscribed as follows: 'King, leaving you was sad and wrong. Peace.'

MORE WAR MEMORIALS — UK

Dartmouth Park Unveiled in April 2011 after the fundraising efforts of local people. Dartmouth Park, St Andrews Avenue, Morley, Leeds LS27 0JX.

Eastriggs Pyramidal monument with carved animal drawings and inscriptions. Devil's Porridge Museum, Stanfield, Annan Road, Eastriggs, Annandale and Eskdale, Dumfries and Galloway DG12 6TF.

Memorials at the National Memorial Arboretum Including: Army Dog Unit (Northern Ireland) Association Red Paw Memorial. Croxall Road, Alrewas, Burton-on-Trent DE13 7AR.

The Animals War Memorial Dispensary Frieze on the facade of RSPCA building, 10 Cambridge Avenue, North Maida Vale, London NW6 5BA.

Bamse (see Chapter 8).

Jet of Iada Jet was a search-and-rescue dog during the air raids of WWII. He and his handler, Corporal Wardle, recovered 150 people. Jet stayed alongside one trapped women for twelve hours until she was finally rescued. Calderstones Park, Liverpool L18 3JD.

Bob the Squadron Dog Bronze sculpture of Labrador Bob by Marion Smith, representing the mascots

FIGURE 59: Many Dickin Medal recipients are buried here at Ilford.

of Fighter Command squadrons in 1940. Battle of Britain Memorial, New Dover Road, Capel-le-Ferne, Folkestone, Kent CT18 7JJ.

Scottish National War Memorial and Graves of Soldiers' Dogs The inscription upon the memorial reads, 'Remember also the humble beasts that served and died.' One of the dogs buried here is reputed to be the German shepherd, Khan. In 1944, he and his handler, Corporal Muldoon, were sent to the Dutch island of Walcheren to overcome German forces. Unfortunately, their boat was unable to land and while Khan made it safely ashore, Muldoon began struggling in the water. Aware his master was still at sea, Khan swam back out and, despite heavy enemy fire, found his handler, whom he pulled to shore. Edinburgh Castle, Lothian EH1 2NG.

The Old Blue Cross Pet Cemetery These 240 graves occupy the site of former kennels that looked after servicemen and women's pets during the war. The kennels also took in the animals of refugees, such as a red setter called 'Whisky' who escaped with his owners from France. Now beautifully restored and tended, modern-day pet owners can have a plaque installed for their own departed pets. Shooters Hill Road, London SE18 4LX.

MORE WAR MEMORIALS — OVERSEAS

There are a huge number of war animal memorials throughout the world. Here are just a few of the better known or unusual ones:

Guardian of America's Freedom The United States' first national monument recognising the sacrifices of dogs in combat. Lackland Air Force Base in San Antonio, Texas, USA.

The National War Dog Cemetery A memorial to war dogs, mostly Doberman pinschers, who were killed in service with the US Marine Corps during the Second Battle of Guam in 1944 in WWII. Apra Harbor, Guam (see figure 62).

Alabama War Dogs Memorial A tribute to military alert dogs in conflicts including Vietnam. The monument features the names and paw prints of dogs. Alabama Battleship Memorial Park, 2703 Battleship Pkwy, Mobile, Alabama 36603, USA.

Gander Statue of Sergeant Gander, a Newfoundland dog and ex-pet who was awarded a Dickin medal forty-nine years after his death. Gander served in Canada where he helped fight the Japanese. He was killed gathering a grenade that had been thrown towards wounded Canadian soldiers. Gander Heritage Memorial Park, 2-10 Lindbergh Road, Gander, NL A1V 1E4, Canada.

Smoky Smoky was a Yorkshire terrier found in a foxhole by an American soldier during WWII. She became a wartime sensation, backpacking through the New Guinea jungle and visiting injured soldiers. One of the smallest war dogs, Smoky's monument shows her sitting in a soldier's helmet. She can be found on Valley Parkway, Lakewood, Ohio 44107, USA, and Bowen Bridge Road, Grounds, Royal Brisbane Women's Hospital, Herston 4029, Australia.

FIGURE 60: Huge bronze sculptures by David Backhouse form part of this multifaceted memorial, the money for which was raised by animal charities. The memorial aims to honour animals who have served throughout time.

The Pikeman's Dog This interesting memorial commemorates the Pikeman's Dog (known as Wee Jock), a terrier who showed great bravery at the Eureka Stockade on 3 December 1854. As a result of the attack on the miners by Crown forces, five British soldiers and some thirty miners died. The memorial consists of twenty-two large golden stockade posts – representing the number of diggers killed in battle – erected in a triangle behind the bronze statue of Wee Jock. Eureka Street, Eureka Stockade Memorial Park, Ballarat, Victoria 3350, Australia.

Australian War Dog Memorial This monument recognises the contribution by Australian dogs that saved soldiers' lives in Vietnam, Somalia, and elsewhere. Alexandra Parade, Alexandra Headland, Queensland 4572, Australia.

HONOURING OUR UK K-9 LAW ENFORCERS: SOME HEROES WALK ON FOUR LEGS

Just like military dogs, our police K9s have roles that often put them in harm's way. Whether it be sniffing out drugs and explosives, searching for lost people and crime scene evidence, protecting their handlers, or chasing down suspects, these dogs have

been an essential part of our police forces since the formation of the dog section within the Met in 1946.[21]

A quick search on the Internet shows how appreciated and revered these dogs are in countries around the world. In the US, for example, police K9s killed in the line of duty often have funerals with full honours. The services feature processions of servicemen and women and are attended by many hundreds of mourners. Monuments to police dogs can be found in every US state and number in the hundreds.[22]

In Australia and New Zealand too, K9s killed in the line of duty are frequently commemorated with impressive monuments and ceremonies.

So what about the UK? It may surprise you to know that even though we are renowned as a nation of animal lovers, until very recently we had no national monument to fallen police dogs, save for a small plaque at the National Memorial Arboretum. While the plaque is a touching commemoration – featuring the words of Byron for his beloved Boatswain (see Chapter 3) – it might be considered somewhat understated when compared to the grand monuments of other nations.

PC Paul Nicholls, an officer and dog handler with the Essex police for more than fifteen years,

ILFORD ANIMAL CEMETERY
Ilford Animal Cemetery, Woodford Bridge Road,
Redbridge, Ilford, Essex IG4 5PS.

ANIMALS IN WAR MEMORIAL
Brook Gate, London W1K 7QF. The memorial can be
found beside Park Lane, at the junction with Upper
Brook Street, on the eastern edge of the park.

K9 NATIONAL MEMORIAL
Oaklands Park, Chelmsford, Essex CM2 0JJ.

FIGURE 61: Smoky – perhaps the smallest war dog?

certainly thought so. When I spoke to Paul, he opened up about how hard it had been losing his police dog, Sabre, and how he desperately wanted to do something to remember him by. This turned into an all-out quest to create a UK national police dog memorial. Paul enlisted the support of local sculptor John Doubleday to create the statue that features a police officer with two retired PDs – Karly, a German shepherd, and Ludo, a cocker spaniel (see figure 63). Paul was keen to have the handler kneeling to show the mutual respect between human and dog.

On a chilly day in April 2019, in the dog-friendly grounds of Oaklands Park Museum, a large group of police dog handlers, their dogs, and many others gathered to listen to the words of Cressida Dick, Commissioner of the Metropolitan Police Service. The Commissioner spoke of how the police dog role is forever evolving: now, for example, dogs are trained to find digital devices such as mobile phones. She also noted how the dogs are 'fantastic ambassadors for policing', and how people's eyes light up when they see the dogs out and about. She spoke of their canine courage and tenacity and also of their sense of fun and desire to work.

After being blessed by the Bishop of Chelmsford to the strains of *I Vow to Thee My Country* and to the claps of all assembled, the beautiful memorial was unveiled. If you go to see it at Chelmsford, be sure to check out the exhibition in Oaklands Park Museum that showcases the history of British police dogs.

Before we leave the topic of these wonderful dogs, we should briefly consider the legacy of a German shepherd called Finn. In October 2016, while working with Hertfordshire police, Finn was stabbed during a criminal pursuit. Although he recovered and was able to go back to work, it was touch and go for a time. The suspect was subsequently caught, but you may be surprised to hear that he was only charged with criminal damage. This is because police dogs have always been classed by UK law as equipment, much in the same way a car or radio would be. In an effort to change this, a petition was set up by his handler, PC Wardell, proposing that police dogs and horses 'be given protection that reflects their status, if assaulted in the line of duty'. When the petition closed it had reached 130,000 signatures and as a result was debated in parliament.

In April 2019, the bill was passed by the House of Lords and given Royal Assent.[23] Finn, who was present in the public gallery, apparently barked as the law went through. Now attacks on police dogs and horses will no longer be classed as damage to 'property', but as aggravated attacks on a sentient being. The new law, known as Finn's Law, came fully into force on 8 June 2019, marking another fitting tribute to our brave K9s.[24]

A SEARCH-AND-RESCUE HEROINE – BRETAGNE
On 6 June 2016, a much-loved golden retriever called Bretagne (pronounced Brittany) was put to sleep. Bretagne was thought to be the last remaining search-and-rescue (SAR) dog deployed at Ground Zero after the 9/11 attacks and officers from the rescue team lined the path to the veterinary surgery, their heads bowed in respect.

9/11 SEARCH AND RESCUE DOGS
Essex County Search and Rescue Dog Statue, Eagle Rock Avenue & Prospect Avenue, West Orange, New Jersey 07052, USA.
Bretagne's commemorative statue resides at the corner of Cypresswood Drive and Mason Road, Cypress, Texas, USA.

FIGURE 62: A Military Working Dog handler pets the head of his Working Dog, at the War Dog Cemetery located on Naval Base Guam, USA. Twenty-five Marine war dogs gave their lives liberating Guam in 1944.

FIGURE 63 (opposite): PD Bodie seems more than happy to give his approval to the K9 Memorial at its unveiling in April 2019. Bodie's handler, Carrie-Ann, told me: 'Bodie is an all-round amazing dog. I am very grateful to have him as a partner. In his two years on the streets [of Glasgow] he has had a great track record for catching criminals and finding property. Bodie and I have been nominated for a Commendation after Bodie found a suicidal missing person on the moors at 2am – without Bodie's amazing nose it could have been a very different outcome.'

Bretagne was one of about 350 SAR dogs used in the Manhattan and Pentagon attacks. When she and her owner, Denise Corliss, were called up it was their first-ever deployment – what a baptism of fire that must have been. They spent the next two weeks working twelve-hour shifts in which they desperately tried to locate survivors amid the apocalyptic scenes of Ground Zero.

The use of dogs in search and rescue is not confined to human disasters. SAR dogs are also used in tracking and after natural events such as hurricanes, avalanches, and earthquakes. Tracking dogs work with their noses to the ground and need a person's scent, such as a piece of clothing, to work from. Air-scent dogs have their noses in the air. Rather than following a trail, these dogs pick out a scent and trace it to its origin. They may use skin cells, perspiration, respiratory, or decomposition gases for this purpose.

Dogs like Bretagne, who work in urban disaster areas, have to cope with traversing difficult and dangerous terrain. In the case of Ground Zero, this was a sixteen-acre obstacle course of concrete blocks, broken glass, ash, and metal. The dogs thrive on positive feedback, such as when they locate a survivor,

and so when the mission became one of recovery rather than rescue, handlers and firefighters hid in the rubble to give the dogs a living person to discover. The dogs helped their handlers in other more subtle ways too, providing comfort in what must have been the most distressing of conditions.

Many human responders suffered with respiratory and other illnesses after 9/11, but what about their canine counterparts? Bretagne was almost seventeen when she died so her work doesn't seem to have reduced her lifespan. In fact, a study by the University of Pennsylvania found that death and disease rates in Ground Zero dogs were much the same as for civilian animals.[25]

Shortly after she was put to sleep, a monument by the sculptress Lena Toritch was installed in Bretagne's hometown of Cypress. Lena revealed how, at the statue's unveiling, she found out about Bretagne's other special talent. A teenage boy at the ceremony suddenly came up and began hugging the statue. Born with autism, he had long struggled with social interaction. At least until he'd met Bretagne, whose calm presence, it was said, had greatly boosted his confidence and communication skills.

More Service Dogs

Bunkou According to the UK Kennel Club, during the Regency period of 1795-1837 Dalmatians were often seen running with horse-drawn carriages where they would calm the horses and prevent other less well-behaved dogs from running out and spooking them. Soon these 'spotted coach dogs', as they were known, became status symbols, especially those with the most decorative patterns.

It is this history that has led to them being associated with the fire service and while we, thankfully, no longer have to rely on horse-drawn fire trucks, Dalmatians are still occasionally used as mascots for the fire service, especially in the US.

One dog who didn't allow the fact that he wasn't a Dalmatian stop him being a fire service mascot was Bunkou. The story goes that around 100 years ago a firefighter in Otaru, Japan saved a puppy from a house fire. Not being able to find a home for the pup, he was kept at the fire station where he enjoyed eating dried herring – a local delicacy. Bunkou (or

Bun Chan) as he was called, soon started travelling on the truck and attending fires, where he would guard the rope cordoning off the scene by barking furiously at anyone who got too close.

Soon he became famous, featuring in news stories throughout the country. It is said that he lived to the ripe old age of twenty-four (perhaps it was all the herring) and rode the truck over 1,000 times. Outside Otaru City General Museum. Ironaiodori St, Otaru, Hokkaido 0041, Japan.

Ashes to Answers One related use of dogs that may not be so widely recognised is the work of the arson dog. These animals are trained to detect common accelerants at fire scenes where illegal activity is suspected. The National Fire Dog statue (also known as From Ashes to Answers) has helped to increase awareness of the work these dogs do, especially after winning the Washington Post's 'Monument Madness' competition for most popular monument in the US – it even beat Mount Rushmore! Engine Company 2 at 500 F Street Northwest in Washington, D.C., USA.

FIGURE 64: Statue commemorating the life and work of SAR dog Bretagne by sculptress Lena Toritch.

FIGURE 65: Bunkou, looking smart in a polka-dot neckerchief similar to the one he sported in life.

FIGURE 66: Arson K-9 Sadie at the National Fire Dog Monument.

REFERENCES

1. Jones Boyd, R., 2015, *On the History of Dogs in Warfare*, Companion Animal Society Newsletter 26(2), pp.14-20.
2. Lanting, F., *Dogs in the Civil War*, http://www. thedogpress.com/DogSense/Civil-War-Dogs_Lanting-126.asp.
3. Stouffer, C. and S. Cubbison, 1998, *A Colonel, a Flag and a Dog*, Thomas Publications, USA.
4. Alexander, E.S., 2015, *Man's Best Comrade: Sallie and the 11th Pennsylvania*.
5. Imperial War Museum, *15 Animals That Went to War*, http://www.iwm.org.uk/history/15-animalsthat-went-to-war.
6. Terhune, A.P., 2013, *A Book of Famous Dogs*, Read Books Ltd., Redditch.
7. Roberts, P., Purr 'n' Fur, http://www.purr-n-fur.org.uk/famous/simon.html.
8. Kean, H., 2017, *The Great Cat and Dog Massacre*, University of Chicago Press.
9. Kennedy, M., *Pet Heroes Honoured as Cemetery Reopens*, Guardian, 14 December 2007.
10. Dog World Magazine quoted in Campbell, C. and C. Campbell, 2016, *Dogs of Courage: When Britain's Pets Went to War 1939-45*, Corsair, London.
11. Campbell, C. and C. Campbell, 2016, *Dogs of Courage: When Britain's Pets Went to War 1939-45*, Corsair, London.
12. *Man's Best Friend: WWI Records Show the Valuable Part Dogs Played in War Effort*, Daily Star, 28 November 2013.
13. Copping, J., *The Western Front's Dogs of War Revealed*, The Telegraph, 28 November 2013.
14. *French Bulldog Trench Messenger The Great War 1917* – YMCA, https://www.youtube.com/watch?v=yhbxwWTZavw.
15. Black, D., 2017, *A Brief History of British Army Dogs in World War 1*, Julius-K9.
16. Campbell, C., 2014, *Bonzo's War: Animals under Fire 1939-1945*, Constable, London.
17. Shute, J., *Unsung Heroes: The Brave Dogs Who Fought in WWII*, Telegraph, 26 September 2015.
18. PDSA, PDSA Dickin Medal, https://www.pdsa.org.uk/what-we-do/animal-honours/the-dickin-medal.
19. Kean, H., 2011, *Tales and Representations: Animal Pasts in London's Present*, The London Journal, 36(1), pp.54-71.
20. K9 Storm Incorporated, K9 Storm Patrol Swat Vest – http://www.k9storm.com/vests.
21. British Transport Police, The dog section, http://www.btp.police.uk/about_us/our_history/the_dog_section.aspx.
22. Connecticut Police Work Dog Association website: http://www.cpwda.com/k9_monuments.htm.
23. Finn's Law: Stabbed Police Dog Law Given Royal Assent, 10 April 2019, BBC, https://www.bbc.co.uk/news/uk-england-beds-bucks-herts-47878060.
24. 'Finn's Law' Delivered to Protect Brave Service Animals, Department for Environment, Food & Rural Affairs and The Rt Hon Michael Gove MP, 8 June 2019.
25. Sinclair, L., *How Did Search-and-Rescue Dogs and Handlers Fare After 9/11?*, Psychiatric News, 2 September 2011.

CHAPTER 6

Myth and legend

TRUTH OR DARE?

CLASSICAL GREEK AND ROMAN literature is full of positive stories extolling the intelligence, loyalty, and bravery of dogs. One of the most famous tales comes from Homer's *Odyssey* (800BC). It features the dog Argos, who has been awaiting his master Odysseus' return for over twenty years (dogs must have had quite long lives back then). When Odysseus finally turns up, Argos recognises him instantly and jumps around, tail wagging. Unfortunately, Odysseus must remain distant from his beloved pet so as to conceal his true identity from some evil suitors who are there to steal his wife. Poor Argos is so distraught at this lack of notice from his long-lost master that he lies back down and dies from a broken heart. This type of tragic portrayal of doggy devotion and faithfulness was common throughout the classical period.

But what about cats? Well, in Asian culture the tale of the Beckoning Cat is a famous legend that remains popular today thanks to the little ornaments that are sold the world over (see Chapter 1). In the Islamic world too, cats have always held far greater approval than dogs, no doubt aided by stories of the prophet Mohammed who was a big cat fan (see Chapter 1). While there are exceptions, such as these and the Norse goddess Freya whose loyal felines pulled her chariot, in the West cats have been depicted much less favourably.[1]

Some of the earliest known cat stories from the western world are thought to be Aesop's fables that date from around 500BC. In these the cat is depicted rather like Tom in the *Tom and Jerry* cartoons – crafty, dishonest, and ultimately losing out to the cannier mice.[2]

During medieval times, the cat continued to be typecast as villain, both in books and real life, while dogs were the personification of loyalty. In medieval paintings of married couples, for example, a dog laid at the foot or in the lap of the lady would symbolise marital fidelity. While in portraits of widows, a dog would represent her continuing faithfulness to her late husband. And western folklore from the 1600s asserted that cats would happily suffocate new-born babies by sucking out their breaths![3]

There have also long been associations between cats and luck. Black cats are thought to be portents of doom in the US, but, conversely, bringers of fortune in the UK. (Sadly, many black cats themselves are not so lucky, with a number of shelters reporting people unwilling to adopt them, apparently due to a perception that they don't photograph well in people's selfies.[4]) It is interesting to note that even today dogs are often depicted as the heroes in films while cats are given roles where they are either evil or the much-loved pet of an evil malefactor. Who can forget, for example, the wonderfully wicked duo of Dr Evil and Mr Bigglesworth in the film *Austin Powers*?

One early tale in which the cat, while still a trickster, was nonetheless clever, resourceful, and of great assistance to his master is that of Puss in Boots. The story appears to have first been published in Italy in 1555 and would go on to influence those prolific master storytellers – the Brothers Grimm. It featured in the hugely popular Mother Goose tales, published in the UK in 1697, and is, of course, still popular

FIGURE 67 (above): The incomparable Puss in Boots.

FIGURE 68 (below): The Whittington Stone pub and Whittington Hospital can be found near Whittington's cat statue in London (see figure 5).

PUSS IN BOOTS
Tuileries Garden, 113 Rue de Rivoli, 75001 Paris, France.

DICK WHITTINGTON'S CAT
See (and hear) Dick Whittington's cat at 53 Highgate Hill, London N19 5NE. And see the man himself with his pet at the ambulatory of the Guildhall Art Gallery, Guildhall Yard, London EC2V 5AE.

today, having been introduced to a whole new generation of fans via the eponymous Dreamworks film.

There are a number of statues worldwide commemorating the savvy and resourceful Puss in Boots, including one in Paris that seems to capture perfectly his rakish, self-confident air.

WHITTINGTON AND HIS EXEMPLARY CAT

Perhaps the most complimentary early tale of a cat is that of Dick Whittington. This story is thought to date back to the late 1300s and involves a destitute young man travelling to London with his cat to earn his fortune. Unable to find work and no doubt bitterly disappointed to find the streets not paved with gold as he had been promised, he decides to return home, but as he climbs Highgate Hill he hears the Bow Bells ringing and it seems they have a message for him:

> Turn again, Whittington,
> Once Lord Mayor of London!
> Turn again, Whittington,
> Twice Lord Mayor of London!
> Turn again, Whittington,
> Thrice Lord Mayor of London!

Once back in the Big Smoke, our Dick embarks on various adventures, including one on a ship where the rat-catching abilities of his cat are much admired. Eventually he falls in love, finds his fortune, and does indeed become mayor three times – a perfect ending.

Well, so goes the story. In fact, although Richard Whittington was a real person, he was certainly not poor (his father was a Lord) and he probably didn't have a cat. Furthermore, while he was indeed Lord Mayor of London, he actually held this office four times, not three. So where did this rather inaccurate tale come from?

FIGURE 69: The endearing statue of a pensive, smiling Whittington with his ever-loving cat. Interestingly, one of Whittington's many legacies went to fund London's first-ever public library located near the Guildhall Art Gallery where this statue is set.

FIGURE 70 (opposite, left): Latvian contemporaries of the Bremen musicians (Riga, Latvia).

FIGURE 71 (opposite, right): The Bremen Musicians, looking friendly – all be it in a slightly threatening way.

It is true that Whittington travelled to London seeking work. His mother had given him the contact name of a mercer (a trader in cloth) who had agreed to take the lad on as an apprentice.

Fast-forward twenty years and we find that Whittington has become very successful, both in trade and in politics. This wealth and prestige continued to grow right up until his death, when he bequeathed huge amounts of money to the city. He donated to enterprises such as houses for the poor, drainage schemes, prison rebuilds, and work on Westminster Abbey. He is also credited with funding various firsts for the capital such as the city's first drinking fountains, its first public library, and even its first public toilets – at least since the Roman times. These gifts made Whittington famous and soon stories were being concocted about him, including and most famously the one told above. As with the tale of Puss in Boots, the story went on to become a much-loved pantomime that still does the rounds every Christmas in Britain.

Incredibly, the charity established to oversee Whittington's money remains in operation today (over 600 years on) and is currently providing homes for the elderly. There is also a large hospital named after the famous mayor in Highgate.

Given this impressive legacy and the enduring appeal of the story, it's not surprising that there are a few statues dedicated to Richard and his cat in the capital. One by Laurence Tindall may be found in the ambulatory at the front of London's Guildhall Art Gallery. And back in 1964, a statue of Dick's cat was placed on the so-called Whittington Stone that was erected in 1821, replacing an even older one. This large stone stands on the site of a former

wayside cross at the foot of Highgate Hill, where, in the story, the distant Bow Bells call young Dick back to London. This statue (see figure 5) is now one of London's twenty-seven talking statues, and if you swipe your mobile phone over the plaque you will hear it come to life with the voice of actress and comedienne Helen Lederer. 'Am I myth or truth?' asks the cat (Helen). 'Did I make my master's fortune?'

On his excellent website,[5] Patrick Roberts considers what many of you may be thinking – just why was a cat associated with the tale given that there is absolutely no evidence that Whittington ever had one? Well, there are a few interesting theories put forward to explain this. One possibility is that it was because Whittington used a type of boat known as a cat in his work as a trader. Another suggestion is that the association relates to the French word *achat*, meaning to buy or purchase. Maybe the answer is simpler: Whittington did indeed have a cat, or maybe it's just that this story, as with many things in life, was simply thought to be improved by the presence of a feline.

A Pyramid of Pets

In the lovely medieval town of Bremen in Germany stands a very unusual statue. Depicting a donkey, dog, cat, and rooster positioned atop one another with the donkey at the base and the rooster at the top, it is based on the folktale known as the Bremen Town Musicians by the Brothers Grimm. Even today there can be few German children not familiar with the tales of the Brothers Grimm and without a collection of their stories in their homes.

Rather strangely, despite the story's title, none of the animals play music and they never actually arrive in Bremen, but no matter, it is still a sweet tale. Probably the most famous version starts with the animals, who are all a bit past their prime, worrying that they're about to be done away with by their owners. Concerned for their futures, they decide to escape to the liberal and artistic city of Bremen where they can form a band and earn their living making music.

As night falls the animals spot a cottage in the woods that would be a perfect place to rest for the evening, but peering in at the window they see that it has been taken over by burglars who are feasting on their ill-gotten gains. Undeterred and rather hungry, they hatch a cunning plan to scare the robbers away.

The donkey beckons the dog up onto her back. The cat then climbs onto the dog and the rooster takes position on the cat. Then, on cue, the donkey brays, the dog barks, the cat meows, and the rooster starts crowing for all he's worth. The robbers are terrified at the bizarre apparition at the window and flee for their lives.

Later, the robbers have second thoughts, no doubt regretting leaving all that yummy food behind and putting the whole sorry experience down to too much alcohol. They decide to go back to the cottage and one of their number is 'volunteered' by the others to check things out. Well, the unfortunate fellow is immediately set upon by the animals; he is scratched by the cat, bitten by the dog, kicked by the donkey, and deafened by the screeching rooster. After this, the four animal friends are left to themselves and rather than travel on they decide to live together in the cottage, no doubt happily ever after.

BREMEN TOWN MUSICIANS
The original statue can be found outside the Rathaus, Am Markt 21, 28195 Bremen, Germany. There are also statues modelled after the Town Musicians in front of each of the five German veterinary schools.
More Bremen Musician representations can be found in various locations in Bremen: Bottcherstrasse's Seven Lazy Brothers is a stone relief and the seven lazy brothers fountain features the animals lined up along the water pipe. There is an ornate wrought-iron bracket extending from the Deutsche Haus featuring the animals. See also Paul Halbhuber's wind rose outside the Kuehne and Nagel Building.
The Latvian sculpture can be found outside St Peter's Church, Skārņu iela 19, Centra rajons, Rīga, LV-1050, Latvia.

GELERT MEMORIAL
Grave of Gelert, Main Street, Beddgelert, Snowdonia National Park, LL55 4YB, Wales.

FIGURE 72 (opposite): The grave dedicated to Gelert is set amid some spectacular countryside.

The moral of the story, I guess, is that you can achieve great things if you work together – even if, like cats and dogs, you don't always get along. Or, as many believe, perhaps the tale and the statue are a symbol of freedom from oppression. This was certainly something that would have resonated with the statue's sculptor – Gerhard Marcks.

Marcks was born in Berlin in 1899 and dedicated his early career to art and its teaching, but in 1933 the Nazis declared his work to go against the beliefs of National Socialism and he was dismissed from his teaching post. Then, in 1937, he was forbidden from exhibiting his work.

After the war, Marcks took up work as a freelance artist and it was then that he was commissioned by the Bremen Tourism Union to create the statue of the town musicians. In 1952, Marcks died. He is considered one of Germany's most influential sculptors.

If there is some debate as to whether there is a political message behind the German statue, it seems likely this is the case regarding a similar monument to be found in Bremen's twin city – Riga in Latvia. Created by Krista Baumgaertel, the work was given to the city by the people of Bremen and is said to have been inspired by Mikhail Gorbachev's perestroika. Rather than staring through the window at the Burglars' feast, the group of animal friends here are peering through the iron curtain. The sculpture was erected in 1990 – just a year before Latvia regained independence from Russia.

BEDDGELERT AND THE MYTH OF THE MARTYRED DOG

When I was a little girl I didn't have a book of Grimm's Fairy Tales, but I did have a similar compendium of stories that was passed down to me from my mother. Much as I liked reading the tales, there was one that always made me cry. This was the famous Welsh story of the Irish wolfhound Gelert and you can find it written on a stone tablet beside a small cairn of stones that are said to mark the noble creature's grave. The inscription goes as follows:

In the 13th century Llewelyn, prince of North Wales, had a palace at Beddgelert. One day he went hunting without Gelert, 'The Faithful Hound', who was unaccountably absent.

On Llewelyn's return the truant, stained and smeared with blood, joyfully sprang to meet his master. The prince alarmed hastened to find his son, and saw the infant's cot empty, the bedclothes and floor covered with blood. The frantic father plunged his sword into the hound's side, thinking it had killed his heir. The dog's dying yell was answered by a child's cry.

Llewelyn searched and discovered his boy unharmed, but nearby lay the body of a mighty wolf which Gelert had slain. The prince filled with remorse is said never to have smiled again. He buried Gelert here.

Every year people visit this grave in the village of Beddgelert (translated from the Welsh meaning

'Grave of Gelert') and read this tale, no doubt some with a few tears brewing. Is the story true though?

Well, as a little girl I suspect I would have been relieved to discover that it isn't. It's a tale that appears, with small variations, in the folklore of countries all over the world and has done so since at least AD540[7] when a version was found in the Sanskrit Indian book – the *Panchatantra*. This incarnation of the tale involves a Hindu family and their pet mongoose. The mother asks her husband to look after their baby son while she fetches water, but instead he goes out begging. In the meantime, a black snake enters the home and, recognising the danger to the child, the brave mongoose kills it. When the mother returns and sees the mongoose covered in blood, she rashly assumes it has attacked the child and hurls her water jar at it, killing the poor, faithful mongoose, before realising her mistake.

Other versions include a tame bear protecting his master's daughter from a tiger in Malaysia and a German father so stricken with guilt at mistakenly killing his courageous dog that he disembowels himself.[8]

The lesson behind all these stories seems to be not to judge a situation too quickly, especially in the heat of passion. (Or alternatively, that it's rarely wise to leave a small child alone in a place frequented by dangerous animals!)

So how did the Beddgelert grave get there? Rather than being from the thirteenth century when the story says Gelert was killed, the cairn of stones marking his grave are actually less than 200 years old. According to a guidebook published in Wales in 1899, *Bedd Gelert: Its Facts, Fairies and Folklore*, it seems they were the brainchild of David Prichard, a landlord of the nearby Goat Hotel.[6] Mr Pritchard had an idea for increasing the tourist trade to the area and his hotel. Knowing the ancient legend of the martyred dog, he reinvented it to fit in with the village, calling the dog Gelert to match the village's name and introducing Llewelyn into the story because of the Prince's connection with the nearby abbey. So, rather than Prince Llewelyn being the one to build the cairn of stones, it was Pritchard, ably assisted by the parish clerk, who was also in on the trick.

FIGURE 73: Close-up of Gelert in Beddgelert, North Wales.

In this case, how do we explain the name of the village? Well, it seems that this most likely derives from a Christian saint called Celert who was living and working in the area around the eighth century.[7] The circumstances of his passing are lost to the mists of time, but what we can say is that Mr Pritchard was a pretty shrewd businessman. Today, some 200 years after he came up with the idea, people travel from all over the world to see Gelert's grave.

THE MOST FAMOUS OF THEM ALL? GREYFRIARS BOBBY
Type the words 'dog statue' into a Google image search and up pops Greyfriars Bobby – a cheeky-looking Skye terrier who is perhaps the most famous of all loyal dogs.

According to Jan Bondeson, who has written an incredibly well-researched account of the little dog's story, around 220,000 people visit Bobby's statue in Edinburgh every year, compared to a mere 20,000 who visit Greyfriars church itself.[8] This popularity was evident as I struggled to photograph the statue in September 2017 amid the enthusiastic crowds gathered around it.

In the book of Bobby's story by Forbes Macgregor, *Greyfriars Bobby: The Real Story at Last*,[9] Bobby is reported as belonging to a man called John Gray who came to the city with his family and became a policeman. In the mid-1800s, Edinburgh was suffering from around 400 deaths a year due to tuberculosis and sadly Mr Gray succumbed to the illness himself in 1858. He was buried in Greyfriars Kirkyard (Kirkyard being a Scottish word for churchyard). According to the legend, Bobby refused to leave his master's grave, staying there in all weathers for fourteen years until he died. For many decades the story has attracted attention around Britain and beyond, being turned into books and films. However, seeing as the story is included in our chapter on myths and legends, you may be surmising that all is not what it seems . . .

In his look at the story, Jan Bondeson tries to determine its authenticity by going through historical sources from around Bobby's time. It seems that the little dog first came to light in a court report featured in *The Scotsman* newspaper of April 1867. It clearly being a quiet time for news, the paper reported on a summons relating to the non-payment of dog tax. This tax was introduced in Edinburgh to try and reduce the number of stray dogs on the streets. The idea was that owners had to license their dogs and pay a fee and any dogs not having homes would be put down.

FIGURE 74: Bobby the little terrier himself atop his Victorian marble column in Edinburgh.
His nose has been worn shiny by people touching it, but sadly this is damaging the statue.

The case was brought against John Traill, the owner of a coffee house at 6 Greyfriars Place, which is just outside Greyfriars churchyard. At one o'clock each day, a gun at Edinburgh castle would fire and this was the cue for Bobby to head down from the graveyard to Traill's café for his lunch. This was something the dog had been taught to do by Sergeant McNab Scott, a military man living close by.

During the court case, Traill explained that although he would pay the tax if pressed, he didn't believe he should have to since he didn't actually own Bobby. He wasn't sure who, if anyone, did, although it seemed the terrier could once have been the property of a certain John Gray, who was buried in the churchyard and whose grave Bobby seemed reluctant to leave.

At this point in the proceedings, the deputy town clerk piped up to say that he had also seen the dog in the churchyard. Then the curator of Greyfriars, James Brown, noted how he remembered the funeral of this John Gray and how the little dog seemed to have started residing in the cemetery just after it. James Brown, despite being a poor man, said he would pay the tax himself, as he wouldn't want to see the loyal little dog done away

with. In the end, however, the court agreed that as it was impossible to fix ownership, the case should be dismissed.

Had no one been in court to report on the case, Greyfriars Bobby may never have become more than a local novelty. As it turned out, one of those reading the story in the newspaper was none other than the Lord Provost, William Chambers. A popular city leader and a confirmed dog lover, Chambers was also director of the SSPCA (Scottish Society for the Prevention of Cruelty to Animals). Mr and Mrs Chambers decided to meet this special little dog who was so faithful to his departed owner, and were so impressed by him that they paid his licence fee and had a collar made. A brass plate upon the collar was engraved with the words: 'Greyfriars Bobby from The Lord Provost, 167'. License and collar can still be seen at the City of Edinburgh Museum in Canongate.

After all this attention, Bobby became even more famous and as his celebrity increased, so too did the numbers of people coming to see him. People were particularly keen to witness his one o'clock trips down to Mr Traill's coffee house, where no doubt many would have stopped themselves to imbibe some

FIGURE 75: Greyfriars Bobby pub is in a Georgian house adjoining the historic Candlemakers' Hall (1722).

refreshment. Soon a number of famous artists came to paint Bobby's likeness, and a postcard featuring one of these pictures and Bobby's story was produced for people to buy as a souvenir from a shop near the church.

Next to play a part in the story was the wealthy Angela Burdett-Coutts who was a leading member of the ladies' section of the RSPCA and a keen London philanthropist. One of Angela's many projects involved the creation of public water fountains for people and animals in London and the Home Counties. On a visit to Edinburgh, Angela met Greyfriars Bobby and was highly taken with the reports of his loyalty in keeping vigil over John Gray's grave. The RSPCA ran a large number of stories about Bobby's fidelity in their magazine, *Animal World*, and there is no doubt that the little dog was helpful in promoting their message to treat animals with kindness.

Burdett-Coutts was so enamoured with the little dog that she commissioned a celebrated sculptor named William Brodie to create a bronze likeness of Bobby to go atop one of her Westmorland granite drinking fountains. After obtaining permission from the council, the statue was duly unveiled in 1873. (A similar one was created in 1904 in London for the 'little brown dog' (see

Chapter 1) and a paper by Hilda Kean presents an interesting analysis of the different ways both statues have been viewed.[10])

The inscription on the fountain reads as follows:

A tribute to the affectionate fidelity of Greyfriars' Bobby. In 1858, this faithful dog followed the remains of his master to Greyfriars' Churchyard and lingered near the spot until his death in 1872.

So why did the story strike such a chord with so many of those who heard it? Well, the idea of canine faithfulness seems to be embedded in our psyche. Ask a group of people what characteristic they most associate with dogs and it's likely a fair few will say loyalty. As we saw in Chapter 2, tales recalling the fidelity of dogs abound the world over.

In his book, Bondeson recalls the stories of a great many so-called cemetery dogs.[7] Like Bobby, these dogs were thought to be keeping vigil on their master's grave for years, but further investigations have revealed that they were much more likely to have remained at the cemeteries due to the food and attention they were receiving. None of these dogs are as famous as Bobby and many have been forgotten. It

FIGURE 76: Bum, Bobby's San Diego cousin.

is no doubt due to Angela Burdett-Coutts' wonderful monument that the wee terrier's story has been kept alive and is still so popular.

So was Bobby just another one of these cemetery dogs? It seems more than likely. Dr Bondeson believes he was simply a stray who was so well treated by James Brown and others at Greyfriars that he decided to stay. In truth, much of the information passed down about him seems a tad dubious. For a start, as we know, he was featured in a number of photographs and paintings early on. As Bondeson notes, the dog shown in these early pictures looks quite different from the one depicted in later paintings and indeed the dog portrayed in the statue. One obvious inconsistency is that the early dog had up-pointing ears! Is it possible that the first dog died and, alarmed at the loss of trade to the café and the drop in sales of the souvenir postcards, John Traill and the church curator James Brown got hold of a new dog to replace him? Bondeson certainly thinks so.

Furthermore, far from 'lingering at the spot' of his master's grave as the inscription on the monument states, Bobby was often seen sauntering around the district, visiting various local businesses for attention and snacks, including the odd piece of steak.

In many ways it is heartening to know that both dogs seem to have lived happy lives rather than a sad existence consisting primarily of pining for a long-dead master. Of course, just because Bobby and similar dogs may not have been in permanent mourning certainly does not mean that dogs can't show a strong attachment to their owners and experience grief at their passing. However, it does seem unlikely that they would continue to associate their dead owners with a gravestone for years on end.

An interesting aside to Bobby's story is its association with another dog statue in the US. In 1978, Edinburgh was twinned with San Diego and the Lord Provost gave the mayor of the Californian city a bronze copy of Greyfriars Bobby. After a few years sitting outside the mayor's office, this Bobby was installed in Gaslamp Quarter Park beside San Diego's own celebrity dog, Bum. Bum was so-named because . . . well, basically because he was a bit of a bum, going round picking fights, cadging food, and even drinking alcohol. It was during an altercation with a bulldog that he was hit by a train, losing half his right foreleg. Despite not getting on with other dogs, he loved people and they loved him.

In 1989, Bum and Bobby were declared 'brother dogs' and a copy of Bum's statue was shipped to Edinburgh. The Americans very much hoped that Bum would be installed next to Bobby, but Edinburgh council weren't so keen on the idea, partly due to

GREYFRIAR'S BOBBY AND BUM

Bobby's statue can be found at 21 Candlemaker Row, Edinburgh EH1. His grave is at Greyfriars Kirkyard, 1 Greyfriars, Edinburgh EH1 2QQ.
Bum can be found at the King's Stables Road entrance to the Princes Street Gardens, Edinburgh EH1 2JY.
Bum and Bobby can also be found at 410 Island Avenue, San Diego, CA 92101, USA.

LA LEGENDE DES CHATS

See the cats in La Romieu 32480, France. Thank you, La Romieu Tourist Board, for giving permission to reproduce the legend here.[11]

Figure 77: Roaming in La Romieu.

lack of space, and possibly, according to Bondeson, because they didn't want this obscure American reprobate anywhere near their saintly Bobby. Instead, Bum can be seen lying at the entrance to Princes Street Gardens, somewhere that was still a part of Bobby's stomping ground.

Bobby himself (i.e. Bobby number 2) is buried inside the churchyard at Greyfriars where, in 1981, The Dog Aid Society of Scotland unveiled a granite memorial to him. When I visited, I watched a group of Japanese tourists add a red ball to the pile of sticks and dog biscuits that lay by the gravestone. Bobby merchandise can be bought at a little shop inside the cemetery, and in the Greyfriars Bobby pub more Bobby memorabilia is on show.

La Romieu

La Romieu is a small picturesque village north of Gers in Gascony, south-west France. It boasts a beautiful fourteenth-century collegiate church, but if you are a cat lover there are many more reasons to visit, for on the window sills, walls, and pillars are stone representations of La Romieu's many cats.

These lovely statues commemorate a medieval legend associated with the village. The star of the story is a little girl called Angeline who was what today we would refer to as a 'crazy cat lady'. She loved cats very much and there were a lot of them wandering the streets of La Romieu.

During the period from 1342-44, La Romieu experienced a spell of very bad weather. The crops failed and before long people were getting hungry. So hungry that the cats roaming the streets were starting to look appetising. One by one the unfortunate felines were killed for food by the starving villagers. Seeing what was happening, Angeline kept her favourite cats hidden in her attic.

Eventually the weather improved and the farmers were able to grow and harvest their crops. However, now they had a new problem: due to the lack of predators, the numbers of rats and mice had grown and were threatening to destroy the harvest.

Luckily, during the time Angeline had hidden her cats away, they'd had kittens. Angeline let loose her cats amongst the rodents, thereby saving the harvest and becoming an instant heroine. It is said that over time the little girl grew more and more to resemble a cat herself and there is a half-cat/half-girl statue of Angeline taking pride of place in the village square.

The statues are the work of Maurice Serreau, who settled in La Romieu for his retirement. In the early 1990s, he began carving the cats, which he offered to various traders in the village. He had been inspired to revive the legend after he had heard it told by a local grandmother to her grandchildren.

WAGHYA
Raigad Fort, Maharashta 402305, India.

'When I look into my dog's eyes, I see worlds and eons that I can touch nowhere else in my modern life.'

Stephen Budiansky

FIGURE 78: The cat-girl Angeline.

WAGHYA – AN INDIAN DOG CONTROVERSY

While La Romieu is certainly pretty, the award for pet statue in the most dramatic setting might well go to Waghya.

Waghya was a sight-hound who is arguably the most famous dog in Indian history. He was said to be the constant companion of Shivaji Maharaj who founded the vast Maratha kingdom, thereby re-establishing rule after the area had been dominated by Muslim dynasties for hundreds of years. Shivaji was crowned Sovereign of the Maratha Kingdom in 1674 and went on to establish a progressive civil administration.

When Shivaji died in 1680, he was given a lavish Hindu funeral culminating in the burning of his body atop a funeral pyre. The legend states that his dog Waghya was so distraught at the death of his master that he leapt onto the burning pyre himself.

In 1936, this act of self-immolation was commemorated with a statue to Waghya, which was erected on a stone pedestal beside Shivaji's tomb. The tomb and statue are found in the remote and scenic mountain fort of Raigad that was once the capital of Shivaji's kingdom.

While the veracity of Waghya's tale is in doubt, the story has become ingrained in modern Indian culture and the name Waghya has become synonymous with loyalty. The statue is not without its critics though. In 2011, the Maratha organisation The Sambhaji Brigade demanded that it be taken down as they maintained that there was no historical evidence to support the existence of the dog and they believed that the statue belittled the Maratha king. Then in August 2012, activists from the Sambhaji Brigade removed the statue and threw it into the valley below. The police arrested seventy-three people in connection with the incident and with the help of locals successfully retrieved the dog's statue and reinstalled it.[12] As of time of writing the statue remains in place.

The story is in some ways reminiscent of that of the Brown Dog statue in Battersea (see Chapter 1) and goes to show that animal statues can still cause passions to run high.

MORE FICTIONAL PET STATUES

A Dog of Flanders A Dog of Flanders is the name of a nineteenth-century novel by English author Marie Louise de la Ramée. Set in Antwerp, it follows the tale of a boy called Nello and his dog, Patrasche, who, homeless and penniless, end up freezing to death in the hallowed halls of Antwerp Cathedral. Not a tale for those who like a happy ending.

However, the book struck a chord with a Japanese diplomat working in the US, who, in 1908, sent some copies home. The translation is now one of the best-known children's stories in Japan and South Korea. It has become required reading for many Asian schoolchildren and was made into a hugely popular TV series and anime film.

FIGURE 79: The statue of Waghya looks particularly impressive in its spectacular landscape.

Strangely, until the 1980s hardly anyone in Belgium knew anything about the tale, but then tourist authorities started to notice that Asian tourists were visiting Antwerp to see the locations in the novel. There are now two statues dedicated to the book. The first, erected in 1985, is a traditional bronze figure of the boy with his dog. Then, in December 2016, a new monument was revealed outside the cathedral. It consists of a marble sculpture of Nello and Patrasche sleeping, partly covered by a blanket of cobblestones, and is possibly one of the most unusual and engaging statues you are ever likely to see. Handschoenmarkt, Cathedral of Our Lady, Antwerp 2000, Belgium and Kapelstraat, Hoboken, Antwerp, Belgium.

Dorothy and Toto Oz Park, Chicago, Illinois, USA. Also: 567 E. Cedar Street, Liberal, KS.

Old Yeller Old Yeller is the eponymous dog hero of the 1956 children's novel written by Fred Gipson. Find him just outside the Mason County District Library, 410 Post Hill Street, Mason, TX 76856, USA.

Lassie Interestingly, the original novel by Eric Knight, Lassie Come Home, was set in Yorkshire, England. Knight moved to Texas, however, and it is here that you can find Lassie's statue. Doylestown, Texas, USA.

Dog on the Tuckerbox This monument was unveiled in 1932 by Prime Minister Joseph Lyons as a tribute to pioneers. It was inspired by a bullock drover's popular poem and song, 'Bullocky Bill', which celebrated the life of a drover's dog that loyally guarded his master's tuckerbox until death and holds a special place in Australian folklore. See this famous little dog in the lovely surroundings of Snake Gully, Hume Highway, Gundagai, New South Wales, Australia.

Hairy Maclary and friends The Strand, Tauranga, New Zealand.

Figure 80: The unusual statue to commemorate the tale of *A dog of Flanders* (Antwerp).

Figure 81: The sculptress Brigitte Wuest has brought author and illustrator Lynley Dodd's cheeky Hairy Maclary characters to life, installing them where children can play with the characters and weave them into their own stories. It's a good example of the trend to create statuary that interacts with the environment. Now that statues have come down from their rather grand plinths, it makes it all the more easy for us to get up close and personal with them! A similar (though non-literary) example from the UK is that of Dr Salter's family (see figure 82).

FIGURE 82: Joyce and Dr Salter's cat by the Thames – a true-life tale portrayed in statuary that forms part of its environment. Back in the early 1900's, Alfred Salter and his wife, Ada, set up a free medical practice in Bermondsey, a poor part of London. Sadly, despite helping many families, the Salters were unable to save their own daughter, Joyce, who died from scarlet fever. The set of statues features Alfred sitting on a bench, Joyce and her little cat next to the wall, and Ada, who worked for the beautification committee whose aim was to green the borough, leaning on a spade. Ada is one of only sixteen public statues of women in London (three of which are of the Queen). Author and historian Hilda Kean notes that 'While the child looked of another age, because of her dress, the cat acted as an image "across time"', bringing the past into the present.'[13]

References

1. Oldfield Howey, M., 2004, *The Cat in Magic and Myth.* Dover Publications, USA.

2. Clutton-Brock, J., 2012, *The British Museum Book of Cats,* 2nd edition, The British Museum Press/The Natural History Museum, London.

3. De Vries, A., 1976, *Dictionary of Symbols and Imagery*, North-Holland Publishing Company, Amsterdam.

4. Malnick, E., *Misfortune of Black Cats Rejected in Age of 'Selfie'*, The Telegraph, 29 July 2014.

5. Roberts, P., Purr n Fur website, *Dick Whittington.*

6. Ashliman, D.L., 1998, *Llewellyn and His Dog Gelert*, Pitt.edu.

7. Bondeson, J., 2011, *Amazing Dogs: A Cabinet of Canine Curiosities,* Cornell University Press, New York.

8. Bondeson, J., *Greyfriars Bobby: The Most Faithful Dog in the World,* Amberley Publishing, Stroud.

9. MacGregor, F., *Greyfriars Bobby: The Real Story at Last,* Steve Savage Publishers Limited, UK.

10. Kean., H., 2003, *An Exploration of the Sculptures of Greyfriars Bobby, Edinburgh, and the Brown Dog, Battersea, South London, England*, Society and Animals 11:4.

11. http://www.gascogne-lomagne.com.

12. *73 Held for Removing Shivaji Dog's Statue from Raigad Fort*, DNA India, 3 August 2012.

13. Kean, H., *Replacing the Salter (and Cat) Statue in Bermondsey*, http://hildakean.com/?p=1646.

CHAPTER 7

Outstanding contribution

FEATS OF INTELLIGENCE AND SKILL

IN OUR EVERYDAY LIVES dogs and cats often surprise us with their seeming intelligence and knowingness. I can recall how my cat would often be at the end of the road waiting for me when I returned from work. A neighbour mentioned how he would wander down there ten minutes or so before I was due home. How on earth did he know the time?

Similarly, my dog now seems to sense when my partner is due home, taking up position in the hallway so she can stare intently at the front door. In fact, some studies suggest that dogs can be as smart as your average toddler. Take Chaser the border collie, for example. She has been taught the names of over 1,000 items and can even sort them into groups by function and shape, something children don't learn till around the age of three.[1]

In this chapter we look at dogs and cats that have been memorialised for their special achievements. Sometimes this relates to feats of intelligence, but in other cases it's simply because they've done something amazing – whether that be orbiting the earth, contributing to medical discoveries, or predicting the sex of unborn babies!

SCIENTIFIC ENDEAVOURS
Pavlov and His Dog Factory

In Chapter 1 we saw how the little brown dog statue was a focus of anti-vivisection campaigning, but perhaps the one name that is most associated with experiments on dogs, even now, some 100 years later, is that of Ivan Pavlov (1849-1936).

Pavlov was a Russian scientist famous for work on a type of learned behaviour known as conditioning. He discovered that dogs produced extra saliva when they were offered food and even on seeing the white coats of the scientists who had previously fed them. He is also credited with revolutionising the study of medicine through his application of the scientific method – the repeated collection of data, its analysis, and verification.

Pavlov performed many experiments that would cause an outcry today. His laboratory has been described as a physiology factory with the dogs as machines, and although Pavlov was reputed to be upset when his dogs died, this, it was said, was only because he wished to perform further experiments on them.

According to a painstakingly researched 800-page biography of the man by Daniel Todes of Johns Hopkins University, Pavlov was a far from pleasant person. Todes notes that he was 'a volatile child, a difficult student, and, frequently, a nasty adult' who was angry and rude to his staff.[2]

There are at least three statues relating to Pavlov's dogs, two of which feature the man himself. Depending upon your point of view, you may consider the monuments as fitting tributes to a biologist who undoubtedly made great strides in helping our understanding of physiology. Or you may regard them more as an acknowledgement of the huge sacrifice contributed by dogs in the pursuit of this knowledge. Certainly the statue at the Institute of Experimental Medicine in St Petersburg has a beautiful poignancy about it.

'Pet a cat when you encounter one on the street.'

Jordan B. Peterson,
12 Rules for Life: An Antidote to Chaos

FIGURE 83: This statue at the Institute of Experimental Medicine in St Petersburg features several poignant inscriptions and bas reliefs.

FIGURE 84 (opposite): Monument to laboratory cats.

St Petersburg State University certainly seems to have been the site of numerous experiments involving cats, some of whom, it was reported, managed to escape and could be seen running loose in the University gardens with electrodes protruding from their heads.[3] Thankfully that is not a sight you will see in the city anymore!

For the travelling ailurophile, Russia's cultural capital makes an attractive destination. The city boasts The Republic of Cats café[4] and a cat museum. Plus, if you visit the city's most famous tourist attraction, The State Hermitage, you may well encounter more cats patrolling the Winter Palace. You will know which are the official pets as they apparently each wear a yellow bow.

In addition to the lab cat monument, there are two more feline statues to seek out in St Petersburg. These animals, known as Elisey and Vasilia or the Yelisei cats, are found on the parapets of buildings on Malaya Sadoya Street. In a story reminiscent of the French Legende des Chats (Chapter 6), it is thought that they are there to commemorate the role of cats during the WWII siege of Leningrad. During the siege, the city's food stores were being destroyed by rats. The army managed to bring in a large number of cats, thereby protecting the dwindling supplies.

Nowadays these little cats are a popular tourist attraction and it is said that if you can throw a coin that stays on the parapet your wishes will come true.

Russian Cats

St Petersburg is thought to be the location of the world's only monument to laboratory cats. This memorial features a 1m-high cat on a tall granite pedestal, around the base of which are tributes to felines from prominent figures, such as the scientist Konrad Lorenz and the playwright George Bernard Shaw. At the statue's unveiling in 2002, Alexander Nozdrachev of the Russian Academy of Science, said, 'Mankind should be extremely thankful to cats which presented the world with a great amount of important physiology discoveries.'

Laika the Canine Cosmonaut

From 1951 until 1966, the Soviet Animals in Space Programme sent more than fifty dogs on missions intended to tell us about the effects of spaceflight on living creatures. Happily, and perhaps surprisingly,

PAVLOV
Pavlov's dog statue can be seen at the Akademika Pavlova Street, 12, St Petersburg 197376, Russia, and Kamennoostrovskiy Avenue, 69, St Petersburg 197022, Russia.
Contact first since access is limited.

LABORATORY CATS
This interesting monument can be found on Vasilyevsky Island at the St Petersburg State University campus.

most of these dogs survived and returned home safely – a few going on to become household pets of the scientists involved.

It's interesting that the USSR chose dogs rather than primates, which were favoured by the American space programme. This choice seems to have come about after Russian scientists interviewed circus trainers about the suitability of both species. They were told that monkeys were less emotionally stable, harder to train, and more difficult to handle than their canine counterparts. On leaving such an interview, Oleg Gazenko, one of the scientists heading up the Soviet programme, is alleged to have declared, 'The Americans are welcome to their space monkeys; we're more partial to dogs.'[5]

Those dogs selected for training were strays found on Moscow's streets. Having lived rough, it was thought that they would be hardier and more resourceful than family pets. They had to be good-natured too of course, healthy, and small enough to fit inside the rocket cones. Lyudmila Radkevich, an assistant at the space programme, recalls travelling around the outskirts of Moscow with a tape measure to measure potential recruits.[6]

The dogs went through a gruelling training regime. They had to endure long periods of inactivity in limited spaces, being kept in small boxes for 15-20 days at a time. They were played loud noises to accustom them to the rocket sounds and made to lay on vibration tables. They were put into centrifuges that simulated the acceleration of rockets upon launch, made to sleep in brightly lit rooms, and even propelled from ejector seats from which they slowly parachuted back to earth.

Although not the first dog to be sent on a space mission, Laika is perhaps the best-known canine

cosmonaut. Prior to Laika's flight, many dogs had been sent on sub-orbital missions, often travelling in pairs in case one dog exhibited atypical behaviour. However, Laika was the first living creature to orbit the earth. She was chosen mostly because of her amazing capacity to endure the tests while remaining calm, but her pretty face with its striking markings also made her a photogenic subject for the media.

Laika, whose name translates as Barker in Russian, was launched in Sputnik-2 on 3 November 1957 after much pressure from the Soviet Premier, Khrushchev. During the Cold War, there was intense competition between the Soviets and Americans to make progress in the space race, and Khrushchev desperately wanted to be first to launch a live passenger into orbit. Unfortunately, his eagerness led to the mission being rushed and hence there was insufficient time for the designers to develop a suitable heat shield to protect the spacecraft during re-entry. This being so, it was clear to all involved that poor Laika would not be returning.

For a long time the circumstances surrounding the little dog's death were shrouded in Soviet secrecy. Official Russian reports first suggested that she had run out of oxygen. Then that she been euthanised some days into the flight by being fed poisonous dog food. Not until October 2002 did the truth about her demise finally come to light. In fact, Laika

YELISEI CATS
Yelisei cats: Malaya Sadovaya Street, 8, St
Petersburg 191023, Russia.

LAIKA
Petrovsko-Razumovskaya Alley, 12A, Moscow
127083, Russia. There is also a monument to Laika
at Hartsdale cemetery in the US and a plaque at
Star City – 141160, Moscow Region, Russia.

had died just hours into the flight due to stress and overheating. The little dog had been fitted with electrodes so scientists on earth could monitor her vital signs and these stopped responding when the rockets thermal insulation was torn away, some 5-7 hours after take-off.

Laika's death is thought to have been painful and distressing, and it is clear that there was a good deal of guilt over the mission. At a conference in Moscow in 1998, lead scientist Oleg Gazenko, who trained Laika, is quoted as saying, 'Work with animals is a source of suffering to all of us. We treat them like babies who cannot speak. The more time passes, the more I'm sorry about it. We did not learn enough from the mission to justify the death of the dog.'[7] It is also apparent from other scientists' memoirs and accounts just how fond many of them were of Laika and the other space dogs. Vladimir Yazdovsky, one of the programme's chief scientists, described Laika as 'Quiet and charming.' He even took her home a few days before the launch to play with his children. 'I wanted to do something nice for her,' he said. 'She had so little time left to live.'[8]

In a further touching report, one of the technicians responsible for settling Laika into her container in the spacecraft noted how he and his fellow technicians all 'Kissed her nose and wished her Bon Voyage.'[9]

It is true to say that the mission prompted outrage in the UK and America, with both the National Canine Defence League and the RSPCA feeling that Laika had been sacrificed to Cold War politics, and calling on people to protest outside Soviet embassies.

In her book, *Soviet Space Dogs*, the Russian research scientist Olesya Turkina notes how surprised the Soviets were at this international outrage.[6] To them, Laika was a good and loyal citizen offering herself up for the Motherland. And it is true that she was hailed a hero, with everything from Soviet cigarette packets, to children's books bearing her image, and even lessons in schools that aimed to teach children to respect and be kind to street dogs.

Meanwhile, in space, Laika's body made 2,570 orbits round the earth before disintegrating along with her spacecraft during re-entry into the earth's atmosphere on 14 April 1958.

In 1997, a plaque commemorating Laika was installed outside Star City, the Russian cosmonaut facility. Then, in 2008, almost fifty years after Laika's fateful voyage, a large monument was unveiled solely to her. Striking and unusual in appearance, it features the little dog held in a human hand that morphs into a rocket. It seems a poignant memorial to such a brave and obedient canine heroine.

INCREDIBLE JOURNEYS
Trim: The Most Illustrious of His Race

While the cat Trim did not orbit the earth in a spacecraft like Laika, he did circumnavigate it in a ship. Trim was one of many cats who, despite not being known for their love of water, have made ships their homes. So common has the ship's cat been throughout history that these feline adventurers have probably done a good deal to propagate their kind around the globe. While onboard the cats would have helped deal with the perennial problem of rodents, and while the ship was in dock it's likely some would have disembarked to check out their local surroundings, perhaps deciding they were more suited to terrestrial living.

FIGURE 85 (opposite): Yelisei cat

FIGURE 86: Laika postcard from 1958 with the first three sputniks. Laika was pictured on cigarette packets, tins of biscuits, spinning tops, pin badges, plates, stamps, books and more. Her story was also the top news in countless newspapers around the world. You can see photographs of the many items of merchandise dedicated to the Soviet's four-legged cosmonauts in Oleysa Turkina's beautiful book, *Soviet Space Dogs*.[6]

carried him so far beyond his mark that he fell overboard; but this was far from being a misfortune; he learned to swim and to have no dread of water; and when a rope was thrown over to him, he took hold of it like a man, and ran up it like a cat.

Trim travelled the oceans with his owner, the cartographer and navigator Matthew Flinders. Born in Donington, Lincolnshire, in 1774, it is a shame that Flinders is not better known in the UK. However, he is widely commemorated in Australia, the land he mapped and identified as a continent and whose name (taken from the Latin word meaning southern) he first popularised. There are over 100 statues to Flinders in Australia, second only in number to those of that much-commemorated monarch, Queen Victoria. Flinders is also honoured through the names of a university, bay, mountain range, national park, railway station, and innumerable roads and streets.

So what of his cat? Trim was one of several kittens born to a dam from Stepney, London, on the ship *HMS Roundabout*. He was mostly black with some white markings and soon became a favourite of Flinders, accompanying him on no fewer than three journeys around Australia and one around the world.[10]

The affection Flinders had for this little cat is amply revealed in the wonderfully humorous tribute he penned that was uncovered in the archives of the National Maritime Museum and published in 1973.[11] On Trim's character, for example, Flinders tells us,

In playing with his little brothers and sisters upon deck by moonlight, when the ship was lying tranquilly in harbour, the energy and elasticity of his movements sometimes

In regards to his appearance, Flinders waxes lyrical, recalling,

Being a favourite with everybody on board, both officers and seamen, he was well fed, and grew fast both in size and comeliness. . . . His tail was long, large, and bushy; and when he was animated by the presence of a stranger of the anti-catean race, it bristled out to a fearful size, whilst vivid flashes darted from his fiery eyes, though at other times he was candour and good nature itself. His head was small and round – his whiskers were long and graceful, and his ears were cropped in a beautiful curve. Trim's robe was a clear jet black, with the exception of his four feet, which seemed to have been dipped in snow.

Of course, Trim was not without a few, some might say, typically feline, faults:

Notwithstanding my great partiality to my friend Trim, strict justice obliges me to cite in this place a trait in his character which by many will be thought a blemish: he was, I am sorry to say it, excessively vain of his person, particularly of his snow-white feet. He would frequently place himself on the quarterdeck before the officers, in the middle of their walk; and spreading out his two white hands in the posture of the lion couchant, oblige them to

FIGURE 87: Belka and Strelka envelope cover and pin badge (1960). These two dogs were possibly as popular as Laika, at least in the USSR. On 19 August 1960 they were the first dogs to be sent into orbit and return home safely. When they landed, onlookers rushed to the capsule yelling, 'They're alive! Alive!' This flight paved the way for the first manned spaceflight less than a year later by Yuri Gagarin. Belka and Strelka lived out their lives being cared for at the Space Institute where Strelka went on to have six healthy puppies.

FIGURE 88 (opposite): The unusual and thoughtful monument to Laika.

stop and admire him. They would indeed say low to each other, 'See the vanity of that cat!' but they could not help admiring his graceful form and beautiful white feet.

Unfortunately, neither the story of Flinders nor of Trim was to end well. As Flinders sailed back to Britain in 1803 (and to the wife he had married ten years previously), his ship was shipwrecked on the island of Mauritius. This island was controlled by the French who England was at war with at the time. Suspected of being a spy, Flinders was taken by the locals and held captive for six and a half years. Thankfully, he did at least have Trim to keep him company and was able to work on his General Chart of Terra Australia – a map containing hundreds of place names Flinders chose for his associations with them in Britain. At some point during this time, however, Trim disappeared. This Flinders surmised was due to his being taken by a hungry native for food. Despite the offer of a princely reward for the cat's return, Trim was never seen again.

Thus perished my faithful intelligent Trim! The sporting, affectionate and useful companion of my voyages during four years. Never, my Trim, 'to take thee all in all, shall I see thy like again'; but never wilt thou cease to be regretted by all who had the pleasure of knowing thee. And for thy affectionate master and friend, he promises thee, if ever he shall have the happiness to enjoy repose in his native country, under a thatched cottage surrounded by half an acre of land, to erect in the most retired corner a monument to perpetuate thy memory and record thy uncommon merits.

Flinders was finally released and allowed to continue his journey back to England. Sadly, he lived for only a few more years, dying aged just forty, on the day after the publication of his great work, *Voyage to Terra Australis*. He was buried at St James Church on Hampstead Road, which was demolished in the 1950s to make way for the expansion of Euston station, and so it was believed that the bones of this intrepid explorer lay somewhere beneath one of the platforms. In January 2019, archaeologists working on the HS2 rail link were delighted to uncover the navigator's lead-lined coffin. This will no doubt be gratifying to his descendants, many of whom attended the unveiling of a statue to the captain some 200 years after his death. The statue, by sculptor Mark Richards, shows Flinders in typical working pose, kneeling over one of his charts, Trim at his side. It can be difficult to fully appreciate its beauty, as it is situated on a plinth that is a popular spot for rail passengers to take a rest amid their luggage. However, in some ways it's gratifying to see the commuters joining Flinders and Trim for some much-appreciated time-out before setting out on travels of their own.

FIGURE 89: Captain Flinders
with his ever-affectionate Trim.

FIGURE 90 (opposite): The statue to Matthew Flinders
and Trim taken on a rainy day at Euston station.

Home-Seeking Bobbie

Most of us like to think that should we somehow
become separated from our dogs they would find a
way to get home. I have a suspicion that my own
dog would get run over on the first road she came
to, but even should she develop some newfound
road-crossing ability, I doubt she could match
the miraculous journey completed by Bobbie the
Wonder Dog.

In 1923, the Brazier family lost their dog, Bobbie,
while on holiday in Indiana. They searched high
and low, but reluctantly had to concede defeat and
return home without the two-year-old rough collie
cross. Then, six months later to the day, who should
appear on their doorstep back in Silverton, Oregon,
but Bobbie.

The Brazier's pet dog had travelled an astounding
2,551 miles across the plains and deserts of the
western United States. He had even traversed the
Rocky Mountains, in winter!

Stories of home-seeking dogs and cats are not
uncommon. In 2013, a cat in Florida travelled 200
miles from a holiday flat back to her home. In the
UK, the sheepdog Pero travelled 240 miles from
Cockermouth in Cumbria to his home in Aberystwyth.
Just in case it might be argued that the owners did
not correctly recognise their own pets, the identity of
both was confirmed via their microchips. Of course,
for every pet that finds their way home, many simply
remain lost, but how do those that manage to get
home, sometimes over vast distances, do it?

The truth is we don't know, although scientists
believe there may be a number of sensory systems at
work. Dogs have a highly developed sense of smell,
but there is also evidence that they possess a special
light-sensing molecule called cryptochrome-1 that
regulates circadian rhythms. Researchers are yet to
fully understand the role of this molecule, but believe
it may be associated with the ability to respond to
magnetic positional information. We also know that
dogs and cats are reward-driven and often form strong
bonds with their owners. Their drive to return home
can therefore be all important. It most certainly was
for Bobbie.

Balto and the Race for Life

At the start of 1925, as winter enveloped the remote
Alaskan town of Nome, a two-year-old Inuit child was
struck down with suspected tonsillitis and died. After
a further three children became ill, the local doctor
realised that their illness was not in fact tonsillitis,
but something much worse – diphtheria. Knowing
this disease was highly contagious, the race was on to

get the anti-toxin needed to treat it. Unfortunately, Nome's supplies of the lifesaving serum were out of date, but thankfully a hospital in Anchorage reported that they had the anti-toxin. The only problem was that Anchorage was almost 1,000 miles away.

Supplies of the serum were immediately transported by train to the town of Nenana, but here trains stopped. How could the serum be carried the remaining 674 miles to Nome? Pack ice in Nome's harbour prevented delivery by ship and the extreme weather conditions made transport by air impossible. It seemed there was no other way for it – the serum would have to be delivered by dog sled.

In a feat of considerable organisation, twenty dog teams were mustered to act as part of a relay. On the night of Monday 26 January, the serum, which had been double packed in thick, insulating material, was handed over to team number one.

On 1 February, through ferocious gales and temperatures reaching minus 85, the package finally reached the final dog team and the musher Gunnar Kaasen. Gunnar specially selected the dog Balto to lead this final stretch. Balto was a fairly small, black husky with white front legs and a white chest. At times on the run Kaasen couldn't even see his hands let alone the trail, so thick was the blizzard, but thankfully Balto knew the path really well. Somehow he managed to lead them safely the final fifty-four miles back to Nome.

When the dogs arrived with the serum, just 127 hours after it had left Nenana, it is said that they were too exhausted to bark. Several had even died along the way due to the rigours of the trip and the effects of frostbite, which had also severely affected the mushers.

The US media had been eagerly following the story and the dogs soon appeared on the front of newspapers and in a Hollywood film. So keen were people to meet these special dogs that Kaasen went on a national tour with his team. This culminated in the unveiling of a statue of Balto in New York City's Central Park in December 1925. Created by F.G. Roth, the bronze sculpture is set on a large granite rock and includes a plaque depicting seven

BOBBIE
Bobbie statue, mural, and replica dog house, 200 S. Wave Street, Silverton, Oregon. Grave of Bobbie, 1067 NE Colombia Avenue, Portland, Oregon.

BALTO
Balto's statue, East Drive at 67th Street, Central Park, New York, USA. Also see Balto and Togo at Cleveland Metroparks Zoo, 3900 Wildlife Way, Cleveland, OH 44109, USA.

LAMPO
Via della stazione, Campiglia Marittima, Italy.

FIGURE 91: A small part of the extensive mural celebrating Bobbie's story.

FIGURE 92 (opposite): Balto standing proud in Central Park, New York.

sled dogs and an inscription that reads, 'Dedicated to the indomitable spirit of the sled dogs that relayed anti toxin 600 miles over treacherous waters, through arctic blizzards, from Nenana to the relief of stricken Nome in the winter of 1925 – Endurance, Fidelity, Intelligence.'

After this brief period of fame, things went downhill for Balto and his teammates. They were sold to an unscrupulous man called Sam Houston who owned a small 'dime-a-look' museum of oddities and curiosities in Los Angeles. Houston charged people to go and look at the dogs, which were kept chained up in a small, dark room.[12]

Luckily, one of those who went to see them was Cleveland businessman George Kimble. Kimble was so appalled at the plight of the dogs, who he could see were being neglected and likely abused, that he offered to buy them there and then. The conniving Houston agreed, but only if Kimble could give him $2,000 – a princely sum in 1926.

Undeterred and determined to rescue Balto and his team, Kimble went back to Cleveland and started fundraising. Through local press and the efforts of everyone, from school children to hoteliers, he managed to raise the necessary money in just ten days. The dogs were duly rescued and provided with a far more suitable home at the Cleveland Zoo where they seem to have led comfortable lives and were well

cared for. Balto stayed at the zoo until his death, aged fourteen. His body was preserved by a taxidermist and put on display in Cleveland's Museum of Natural History, where you can still see him today.

The famous serum relay of 1925 is still commemorated with the Iditarod Sled Dog Race that runs from Anchorage to Nome every year. But an even greater legacy of the 1925 run is that it was the start of a global campaign to inoculate people against diphtheria – now a rare disease indeed.

The British Sled Dog Memorial

Just outside the Scott Polar Research Institute in Cambridge, we have our own husky dog monument. This bronze statue, together with a plaque naming the British Antarctic Dog Teams, was unveiled in the summer of 2009. It aims to help us remember the 1,204 British dogs used in Antarctica from 1945-93. Hwfa Jones and Graham Wright of the British Antarctic Survey, two of the men who worked hard to see the statue created, noted that the monument represented 'A thousand personal stories, most of which will never be told in any official documents. These dogs shared in the discovery of the continent from which they are now forever banned.'[13]

This latter statement refers to the withdrawal of the last remaining huskies from Antarctica on 22 February 1994. This was due to a clause in the

Antarctic Treaty that required all non-native species to be removed in order that diseases like distemper would not be spread to the native wildlife.

Lampo the Railway-Travelling Dog

Before health and safety regulations forbid such things, quite a lot of dogs used to live and travel on the railways. Perhaps this is not surprising considering the fact that stations provided the main things dogs require – shelter, warmth, food, and the fuss and attention of staff and customers.

One of the more famous of these commuting canines was Lampo (who was named after the Italian word for lightning due to his speed jumping on and off the engines). Lampo made his base at Campiglia Marittima, an Italian station on the line between Pisa and Rome. It is reported that he seemed to know when the express trains were due and would run onto the platform for the train's chefs to throw out scraps for him. But Lampo soon got bored hanging around the station and began heading out to Pisa, Rome, Florence, and numerous other desirable destinations, seemingly knowing which stations to change at in order to arrive back safely at Campiglia Marittima.

Not everyone was a fan of Lampo. The station master at Campiglia Marittima was definitely not a dog lover and despite protestations from his assistant, Elvio Barlettani, who had originally taken Lampo in,

he placed the dog in a luggage van on a train destined for far away Naples. Lampo would never find his way back from there, he must've surmised, no doubt with an evil grin on his face.

Well, he was wrong. Five months later Lampo appeared again at the station. He was ill and thin, but Barlettani and his staff nursed him back to health. Fortunately, the station master had since been replaced with someone more dog-friendly and Lampo was allowed to stay.

By now Lampo was a bit of a star, even featuring in the US periodical *This Week*. However, just one year later, Lampo, who had become rather old and slow, fell under a train and was killed. *This Week* paid for a statue to be erected to the rail-travelling dog, which, despite rather bizarrely being vandalised by a self-confessed cat lover, remains at Campiglia Marittima station today.

More Well-Travelled Dogs

Red Dog This kelpie cross made many friends in his life riding the buses around his hometown in Western Australia and then, after his bus driver owner died, hitching his own rides! The Red Dog Statue is on the left as you enter the Dampier, Western Australia 6713, Australia.

Seaman In 1804, President Thomas Jefferson sent out an expedition to map and investigate the newly

FIGURE 93: Balto and his teammate Togo playing in the snow at Cleveland Zoo.

acquired territory of the western United States – a huge portion of land stretching from St Louis to the Pacific coast. Led by Captain Lewis and Lieutenant Clark, the group took two years and four months to travel the 3,700 miles there and back. They were accompanied by Lewis' Newfoundland, Seaman, who protected the camp at night from bears and, on one occasion, a rampaging bison. He also caught squirrels that the men cooked up, and even saved one of the group from drowning. Seaman had to endure the attention of plagues of mosquitoes, barbed foxtail seeds that dug into his coat, and even being bitten by an angry beaver! He made it home with Lewis and the rest of the men, and he is now commemorated in a large number of statues throughout the US. 500 S. Riverside Drive, Saint Charles, Missouri 63301; 101 W. Capitol Avenue, Jefferson City, MO 65101; Sioux City Lewis & Clark Interpretive Centre, 900 Larsen Park Road, Sioux City, IA 51103 (see figure 2 at the beginning of the book); and many more . . .

Dogs and Cats Just Doing Their Thing
Towser

As we know, cats have been helping people with their mice problems ever since we started storing grain, but naturally some cats are better in this department than others. The best ever, at least according to the *Guinness*

Book of Records, was a long-haired tortoiseshell called Towser. Towser lived and hunted for twenty-four years in the Glenturret whisky distillery in Crieff, Scotland. Amazingly, she caught 28,899 mice and rats. (No one actually counted these rodents, you may be relieved to hear, rather, the *Guinness Book of Records* recorded Towser's behaviour over several days and extrapolated.) This number means that she nabbed an average of 3-4 rodents every day. Quite an impressive feat and one that might have been assisted by a nightly snifter of the 'strong stuff' in the milk, according to some rumours.

To mark thirty years after her passing, Towser is commemorated in a bronze statue outside the distillery shop. Nowadays cats aren't used to rid Glenturret of mice, but their current two moggies still play an important role greeting the centre's visitors.

Master McGrath

Master McGrath was noted to be a small and weak pup, but this didn't stop him becoming the most celebrated hare-coursing dog of his time. He was a three-time winner of the Waterloo Cup and such a celebrity that Queen Victoria asked to be introduced to him.

Today, we are increasingly becoming aware of the cruelty some greyhounds have suffered at the hands

FIGURE 94: Lampo with his station master hat and signal stick (Campiglia Marittima, Italy).

of racing and related sports. A memorial to some of these can be found at the pet cemetery at Brynford, and you can read more about the campaign to reform the racing industry via the link in the references.[14]

New Zealand's Tribute to the Collie

There are some statues that are stunning partly by virtue of their surroundings and the MacKenzie sheepdog monument is surely one of them. This bronze dog stands proudly atop a mound of granite. His gaze is directed across the turquoise waters of Lake Takepo to the misty mountains of the Southern Alps beyond. A plaque on the side of the statue reads, 'This monument was erected by the runholders of the MacKenzie county and those who also appreciate the value of the collie dog, without the help of which the grazing of this mountain would be impossible. Unveiled on March 1968 by Sir Arthur Espie Porritt, Governor-General of New Zealand.'

Although the statue commemorates the border collie breed rather than any particular dog, it could be argued that it might never have existed were it not for a collie called Friday.

Friday belonged to James MacKenzie who was born in Ross-shire and who, along with many other Scottish shepherds and their collies, emigrated to New Zealand in the 1850s to work on the pastoral runs of South Island. But MacKenzie was to prove to be a bit of a black sheep himself. When he joined the farms he discovered that there would often only be a couple of men working there. With security so lax, he would steal the flock at night by driving the sheep away with Friday, before selling them to other farmers.

The area into which MacKenzie drove these flocks is now known as MacKenzie county, having been named after him. During MacKenzie's time, it was remote and almost uninhabited. Records suggest that MacKenzie got away with hiding his flocks here for several years before the authorities finally caught up with him. After capture, he was held in prison but somehow managed to escape (twice) in an effort, it is said, to be reunited with his dog.

Unfortunately, records are unclear as to what eventually happened to Friday, however both man and dog are commemorated in a statue in the town of Fairlie.

UNUSUAL TALENTS

Jim the Wonder Dog

Born in the 1930s in Louisiana, USA, Jim was a Llewellin setter (rather like an English setter) credited with possessing some spectacular abilities. It is said that he could go out on the street and locate a car by

FIGURE 95: The Red Dog is remembered on the road into Dampier, Australia, where he once lived.

FIGURE 96 (opposite): Towser looking proudly on while two Glenturret kittens
wonder what all the fuss is about.

type, colour, and number plate. He was also able to understand languages, Morse code, and short-hand. As if all that weren't enough, he could even predict the future, including determining the sex of unborn babies and correctly forecasting seven consecutive winners of the annual Kentucky Derby!

Jim, who was owned by a hunter from Missouri called Sam Van Arsdale, performed his amazing feats of intelligence in front of many audiences, including at the Missouri State Fair. He impressed a lot of people. His story may remind you of that of Clever Hans, a famous horse who astounded people in his native Germany by seemingly being able to perform complex mental arithmetic. Hans' owner would give the horse a sum to work out and Hans would reply with the correct answer tapped out by hoof.

In 1907, the German psychologist Oskar Pfungst began a careful study of Hans to try and determine exactly what was going on. Pfungst found that Hans would give the right answer even if he were asked the question by someone he didn't know. However, he could only get the answer right if he could see the person asking the question and if that person themselves knew the correct answer.

With this in mind, Pfungst went on to examine the body language of the questioner more closely. He noticed that as the horse tapped out the answer the questioner's facial expression and posture changed as the correct answer was approached and relaxed when the final tap was made. This, Pfungst believed, was the cue that Hans was using to tell him when to stop tapping. This effect, in which the researcher's involuntary reactions cause them to influence the subject of an experiment, became known as the Clever Hans effect and was an important discovery because it helped prevent unconscious bias in scientific studies. Certainly we know that animals like dogs are very responsive to the little cues we give out in our day-to-day lives (taking their lead out of the drawer, for example), and this is, of course, one of the things that makes them so trainable.

Regardless of the likely scientific explanation for at least some of Jim's incredible talents, he still attracts much affection. Jim has his own website/fan club, and his statue in Missouri is set within its own picturesque garden with a nearby museum dedicated to him.[15]

Advertising Icon
Dogs Don't Listen to Phonographs!

Our last story in this chapter concerns Nipper, a likely mix of Jack Russell and fox terrier, who had a habit of nipping the backs of people's ankles – hence his name. Born in 1884 in Bristol, he seems to have been a stray who was taken in by Francis Barraud who earned his keep as an artist.

Frances noticed how Nipper liked to listen to the phonograph and how he would tilt his head quizzically at it as if trying to work out where the sounds were coming from. However, it was only after Nipper died in 1895 that the artist decided to capture this appealing image in a painting.

Pleased with the result of his labours, Francis submitted the artwork to the Royal Academy for display, but was unfortunately turned down. Similarly, requests to magazines asking them to feature the picture were also refused, and when he approached the Edison Bell company in the US who produced the phonograph, he was informed (rather stuffily) that 'Dogs don't listen to phonographs.'[16]

Poor Francis may well have given up on his picture had not a friend suggested he substitute the black phonograph horn with a more modern and attractive brass one. Thinking it was worth a try, Francis agreed and approached a newly formed gramophone company to ask if he could borrow such a horn to copy. This turned out to be a good move. The company manager was really impressed by Francis' picture and offered to buy it there and then – on one proviso. That Francis replace the whole phonogram with one of the company's brand new, state-of-the-art Berliner disc gramophones.

This Francis duly did and the resulting picture, which he named *His Master's Voice*, was proudly hung in the gramophone company's offices.

In 1900, Emile Berliner, one of the inventors of the gramophone, saw the painting on a visit to the office and was so delighted that he decided to use it as a trademark for the company. Soon the logo and the slogan, 'His Master's Voice', was everywhere. Francis was paid $50 for the copyright and another $50 for the painting. Goodness knows how wealthy he would have been had he retained ownership of the copyright.

Questioned some time later on the painting, Francis is reported to have commented,

It is difficult to say how the idea came . . . beyond the fact that it suddenly occurred to me that to have my dog listening to the phonograph, with an intelligent and rather puzzled expression, and call it 'His Master's Voice' would make an excellent subject. We had a phonograph and I often noticed how puzzled he was to make out where the voice came from. It certainly was the happiest thought I ever had.

The artist would no doubt be almost as happy to know that the trading company HMV (an acronym of the artwork's title) still use his charming painting of Nipper to this very day, albeit in silhouette form.

'If you think dogs can't count, try putting three dog biscuits in your pocket and then give him only two of them.'

Phil Pastoret

FIGURE 97: Jim the Wonder Dog's statue takes pride of place in his own immaculately manicured gardens.

TOWSER
Glenturret Distillery, The Hosh, Crieff PH7 4HA, Scotland.

MASTER MCGRAPH
12 High Street, Lurgan, Craigavon, Co. Armagh, BT67 9DR, Northern Ireland.

JIM THE WONDER DOG
Jim the Wonder Dog statue and memorial garden – 101 N. Lafayette Avenue, Marshall, Missouri 65340.

MACKENZIE SHEEPDOG
Border collie statue, Pioneer Drive, Near Church of the Good Shepherd, Lake Tekapo, New Zealand.
MacKenzie and Friday statue, Fairlie, New Zealand.

GREYHOUND MEMORIAL
The Pet Cemetery, Brynford, Holywell CH8 8AD.

NIPPER
Nipper was buried in a small park in Clarence Street, Kingston-Upon-Thames in Surrey. The park now has a Lloyds bank standing on it, but a plaque inside commemorates the terrier. In 2010, a small road near to the dog's resting place in Kingston-upon-Thames was named Nipper Alley.
Nipper's statue can be seen at the corner of Park Row and Woodland Row, Bristol.
A giant 4-tonne Nipper sits on the roof of the old RCA building, 991 Broadway, Albany, New York USA.

REFERENCES
1. Griggs, J., *Border Collie Takes Record for Biggest Vocabulary,* 21 December 2010, New Scientist.
2. Todes, D.P., 2017, *Ivan Pavlov: A Russian Life in Science*, Oxford University Press, USA.
3. Melvin, J., *City Tales: Divine Felines*, St. Petersburg Times, 23 July 2014.
4. http://www.catsrepublic.ru.
5. Wellerstein, A., *Dogs in Space*, The Nuclear Secrecy Blog, 26 June 2015, http://blog.nuclearsecrecy.com/2015/06/26/dogs-in-space.
6. Olesya, T., 2014, *Soviet Space Dogs*, Fuel, London.
7. *Oleg Gazenko*, Wikipedia.
8. Isachenkov, V., April 2008, *Space Dog Monument Opens in Russia*, MSNBC.
9. Zak, A., *Sputnik-2*, Russianspaceweb.com.
10. Welbourne, D., *Matthew Flinders, Explorer*, Lincolnshire Life, January 2014.
11. Flinders, M., 1814, *A Biographical Tribute to Trim.*
12. Aversano, E.J., *Balto's True Story*, http://www. baltostruestory.net/balto.htm.
13. Antarctic Sledge Dog Memorial – Cambridge, Cool Antarctica.
14. C.A.G.E.D. North West [Campaign Against Greyhound Exploitation & Death] http://www.cagednw.co.uk.
15. Jim the Wonder Dog website, http://www.jimthewonderdog.org.
16. Design Boom Magazine, *The Nipper Saga*, http://www.designboom.com/history/nipper.html.

FIGURE 98: The statue of MacKenzie sheepdog looks out across beautiful Lake Takepo.

FIGURE 99: Nipper looks down on shoppers from his perch near the site of the former Prince's Theatre, Bristol.

FIGURES 100-104 (following page): Now you see us! Just five of the more than twenty cats of York.

CHAPTER 8

Curiouser and curiouser

THE WEIRD AND THE WONDERFUL

OUR FINAL CHAPTER LOOKS at some of the more unusual pet statues – from giant polychrome cats to peeing dogs!

THE CATS OF YORK

If you visit the lovely medieval city of York, you may suddenly notice that there are a lot of cats around. Not real cats, but little statuettes attached to walls, roofs, and window sills. Some peep down at you, a few seem to be stalking you, while others sit tidily on their high-up perches. All make a lovely addition to the city and are in many ways reminiscent of their French counterparts in La Romieu (see Chapter 4).

York's oldest cat statues are believed to have appeared in the 1920s, though there is some uncertainty on this. They reside on a couple of houses in Low Ousegate, opposite the river. At least one of these residential houses was once a grocer's and it is thought that the then proprietor, Sir Stephen Aitcheson, may have added the cats to scare away rats and pigeons.[1]

Perhaps prompted by the existence of these two felines, the architect Tom Adams had the idea to add cat statues to the buildings he designed in the area. Tom was a cat lover who as a student had included pictures of cats in his architectural drawings to give them perspective. He commissioned local sculptor Jonathon Newdick to create the statues from fibreglass, concrete, and later, polyester resin, which is apparently almost indestructible.

Tom added this quirky 'feline signature' to his buildings from the 1980s right up to 2005, not long after which he passed away. It seems that many businesses and homeowners in York have wanted to continue Tom's tradition and there are now around twenty-two cat statues in the city – though the number is somewhat fluid with new cats being added and others being lost and sometimes found again!

Nowadays, visitors to York may download a trail map showing locations of the little statues.[2] It takes around an hour and a half to spot them all – some being obvious, while others are quite a challenge.

CATS OF KUCHING CITY

While York certainly has a wonderfully quirky appeal to cat lovers, Kuching City in Malaysia takes feline obsession to new heights – something that is perhaps not surprising when you consider many believe its name derives from the Malay word for cat.[4]

This feline fascination manifests itself in many ways. Take, for example, the fact that the local radio station is called Cats FM, that there are cat ornaments and T-shirts for sale everywhere, and that the city's crest is a pair of justice scales with a large golden cat atop them. Then there is the Cat Museum housing over 4,000 cat-related artefacts.[5] And of course there is the obligatory cat café – in this case called Meow Meow. But it is the cat sculptures that are perhaps the most eye-catching and these appear on pavements and on rooftops, in parks and in temples. What's more, some of them are enormous.

One of the most imposing of these large sculptures is the Great Cat of Kuching who raises a paw to onlookers from a traffic island by the Chinese

FIGURE 105: The Great Cat of Kuching.

FIGURE 106: Giant playful cat family in Kuching.

ceremonial gate. This 2.5m white cat is bedecked in traditional costumes during festivals – red for Chinese New Year, green during Eid, a Santa costume at Christmas, and a traditional Iban vest during harvest festival.

Equally impressive is the colourful polychrome cat family opposite the Hotel Grande Margherita. Here two giant tabby parent cats sit proudly while around them five cheeky polychrome kittens appear to be getting up to various types of mischief.

But one of the nicest things about Kuching is that there are many living cats too. True, many are a little thin and mangy and it may alarm visitors to see that a fair number have stumpy, deformed-looking tails. However, this does not appear to concern the cats. The most likely explanation for the seeming defect is that it is genetic – possibly as a result of many of Kuching's cats being descended from short-tailed breeds like the Japanese bobtail.

We have seen in other chapters how cats have often been credited with saving towns and villages by protecting food stores from rapidly multiplying rodents. There is a similar story to be told in Borneo, but it stands out for a couple of reasons – firstly in that it is often held up as an example of how interfering with natural ecosystems can have unforeseen and disastrous consequences, and secondly, because it involves parachuting cats!

The story begins in the late 1950s when the World Health Organisation (WHO) began spraying the villages of Borneo with DDT (or, as some sources suggest, Dieldrin).[6] The hope was this would lead to a reduction in mosquito numbers and hence a fall in the incidence of malaria. A short time after the treatment, it was found that the thatched roofs of houses in the area were starting to collapse. The reason was down to a rapid growth in numbers of moth larvae that were eating the roof palms. While the larvae were unaffected by the chemical spraying, the predatory fly that ate them was being wiped out. Worse still, lizards who ate these contaminated flies were building up concentrations of the poison in their bodies and when they in turn were eaten by cats, the cats died. It doesn't take much imagination to work out what happened next: as cat numbers plummeted, so rat numbers rose. The disease-carrying mosquitoes had effectively been replaced by disease-carrying rats.

So it was that in 1960, Operation Cat Drop began. The mission involved the WHO and Singapore Air Force parachuting into the affected villages thousands (some say 14,000) of cats of every description. While it is tempting to imagine the cats descending gracefully from the skies with little parachutes attached directly to their backs (landing expertly on all four paws, of course) it seems the felines were first placed into padded and perforated containers. Some dispute the authenticity of the story and there is little doubt it has been embellished on occasion. However, when WHO staff recently conducted research into the matter they found a quote in the RAF Changi Operations Record Book from March 1960 that stated 'Many thanks to R.A.F. and all responsible for air drop arrangements; also to cat donors and cat basket makers. All cats safe and much appreciated.'[6]

FIGURE 107: The cats on the lawn outside the James Brooke Bistro provide an interesting view for diners.

LOCAL PET CELEBS

For some pets, one owner isn't enough. Some want to belong to a whole community and in doing so they often bring people together in surprising ways. We'll look at some of these 'community pets' next.

Bosco the Mayor

Satisfaction ratings for those holding public office often leave something to be desired, but one town official who everyone seems to have liked was Bosco. Perhaps this was because he was a dog!

Bosco, or Bosco Ramos, to give him his full moniker, was a black Labrador/Rottweiler cross who was elected mayor of the little Californian town of Sunol in 1981. His name was submitted as a joke alongside two more conventional (human) candidates, however Bosco beat them hands down. His electoral slogan, which clearly struck a chord with voters, stated, 'A bone in every dish, a cat in every tree and a fire hydrant on every corner.'[7]

Bosco took well to civic duties. He was known for officiating over the town's events while wearing a smart, custom-made tuxedo vest. For less prestigious events he would don his red bandanna.

It must be admitted, however, that he was often found in local bars appealing for treats (and growling if you didn't give him one).[8] It is also true that he did occasionally go missing on the job, perhaps in order to engage in the odd romantic tryst, to which residents say he was rather partial. Certainly he is thought to have fathered a great many pups in the area.

Bosco's tongue-in-cheek tale is a quaint local story that made world news after being featured in the British tabloid *The Daily Star*. But not everyone saw the funny side. In 1989, following the Tiananmen Square protests, a Chinese newspaper, *The People's Daily*, ran an article on how Bosco's election showed serious flaws with the democratic electoral system. Naturally, after this, Bosco's fame increased further still and he even became the guest of honour during student protests on democracy at the Chinese Consulate in San Francisco.

Bosco remained mayor right up until he died in 1994. Then, in 2008, a statue was erected in his honour by the Russian artist Lena Loritch.[9] The likeness features Bosco's signature neckerchief and seems to capture his happy-go-lucky disposition perfectly.

Monty the Community Labrador

Monty would often visit the shops at Stones Corner with his owner, helpfully carrying the purchases back

'They are fed but not kept as pets; they
roam at will like furry, community
free-range chickens.'[3]

The writer Ricky French on Kuching's cats

BOSCO

Bosco can be found outside Sunol Post Office – 11925
Main Street in Sunol, California. A life-sized stuffed
dog resembling Bosco resides on the bar at the
Western-themed pub, Bosco's Bones and Brew. Like
Bosco, there is more to this dog than meets the eye
since a lift of his back leg results in him dispensing
(urinating) beer for amused/horrified customers.

MONTY

Meet Monty on Logan Road, Stones Corner,
Queensland 4120, Australia.

FIGURE 108: Lena Toritch's statue of Bosco,
the popular dog mayor.

for him in a wicker basket. Monty got so familiar with
this routine that when his owner was busy, Monty
would head down to the shops on his own! The shop
owners would fill out the orders, written on a list in the
basket, and send Monty on his way with the groceries.

Not surprisingly, Monty soon became a bit of a
celebrity, including featuring in the local newspaper,
but this didn't stop him falling foul of a new set
of dog laws brought in by Brisbane City Council.
Having been spotted shopping on his own, Monty
was picked up by the dog warden and taken to the
local pound.[9] Monty was thankfully allowed back
home, but his owner was issued with a warning never
to let him go out alone again. Despite a petition
and various letters on Monty's behalf, the Council
remained unrepentant. Shortly after, Monty and his
owner moved away from Stones Corner, but a statue
of the much-loved dog remains, and of course, it
features him holding his basket of groceries.

Writing on Monty's story, a local blogger notes
how much the town has changed since Monty's time,
with many of the shops boarded up and far fewer
people on the sidewalks.[10] I suspect the real Monty
wouldn't have liked it as much.

Hamish the Community Cat

While local controls may leave no place for a
community dog in our increasingly ordered towns,

cats can still get away with doing their own thing –
often without their owners having a clue what they're
up to.

A story on the Fox News website recounts how
a family often welcomed a cat into their home,
especially in inclement weather.[11] He would have
some food before spending the night on one of
the children's beds. It was only when they were
in conversation with others at a neighbourhood
Christmas party that they found out that three other
families in the area were also welcoming him. That's
four lots of attention and four lots of food!

Such two- (or four-) timing moggies are not
uncommon (and were probably the norm before
WWII in Britain). While many owners may feel a
little peeved at their wandering pet, others have
come to amicable arrangements, such as the families
in New Zealand who have had a shared cat custody
agreement drawn up.[12]

One famous free-range feline was Hamish
McHamish, a ginger cat living in St Andrews,
Scotland. Although Hamish had a good home, his
roaming started when he was barely one year old.
He particularly liked to visit local shops and cafés,
the Holy Trinity Church, and St Andrew's University
buildings, perhaps depending upon whether it was
dietary, spiritual, or intellectual sustenance he was
after.

FIGURE 109: Monty engaging in a bit of retail therapy.

FIGURE 110: Hamish – St Andrew's community cat.

Hamish died in September 2014, but his statue (unveiled a few months before his demise) is a lasting reminder of him.

MORE LOCAL PET CELEBS

Biggles was a schnauzer who used to ride in a milk crate on the back of his owner's motorbike. Despite being small, he had a larger-than-life character and was often seen leaping between balconies in pursuit of cats. Unfortunately for poor Biggles and his many fans, his final leap was off a cliff and to his death. Atherden & Playfair Streets, The Rocks, New South Wales 2000, Australia.

Sam the Cat This statue honours a resident who was very much human, but known for her love of cats. Nurse Patricia (Penny) Penn (1914-92), was much respected in the local community that she helped to protect from developers. Apparently Penny would often credit her ideas to her cat, Sam.[13] Queen Square Gardens, Holborn, London.

Brutus the Morrisons Cat According to staff at the Saltney branch of Morrisons in Flintshire, Brutus the tabby cat would wander from his home to the supermarket every day. Here he would greet shoppers, see what was on offer at the fish counter, and catch a few ZZZs in the baby seats of the shopping trollies. He was so popular that when he

passed away, shoppers raised £4,000 to have a statue of him erected. Morrisons, High Street, Saltney CH4 8RU.

Catford Cat While on the subject of shopping we mustn't forget the Catford Cat – a large fibreglass moggie adorning the Catford shopping centre. A few years ago the council had wanted to remove it, but they were met with a storm of protest. 'It's the best thing about Catford!' they were told in no uncertain terms. Catford, London SE6.

Alfie the Rushden Station Cat According to his beautiful memorial, he 'arrived a stray and departed a legend'. The old railway station, Station approach, Rushden NN10 0AW.

MONUMENTS TO THE HOMELESS

In 1981, a wonderfully quirky sculpture by Professor Siegfried Neuenhausen was unveiled at the intersection of three streets in the German town of Braunschweig. The statue features a steel column interwoven with many bronze cats in a variety of largely mischievous-looking poses. The statue may be in recognition of the name of one of the streets where it stands – Kattreppeln. It is also often known as the Monument to Homeless Cats, and according to some writers, it is a call for people to be more aware of the many strays in the area.

HAMISH
Church Square, St Andrews KY16 9NW, Scotland.

MALCHIK
Just inside Mendeleyevskaya station, Moscow, Russia, 127055.

GIRO
9 Carlton House Terrace, St James's, London SW1Y 5AJ.

JUST NUISANCE
St George Street, Simon's Town, South Africa.

BAMSE
Fiskeriveien, Honningsvag, Norway, and Wharf Street, Montrose DD10 8BD, Scotland.

FIGURE 111: The complicated Braunschweig cat sculpture. It is said few can count the number of cats without getting a headache.

FIGURE 112: (opposite) Malchik who was killed in the station (Mendeleyevskaya station, Russia).

In Russia too there are a number of monuments to homeless animals including some that double-up as ornate and rather beautiful money boxes. The money donated goes to help the local rescue centres. But the most famous Russian monument to strays, and to one homeless dog in particular, was erected at Mendeleyevskaya station in 2007. The statue, called Compassion (or sometimes Sympathy), shows the dog Malchik, a black mongrel who liked to hang around the metro station and was well known to the local shops and rail employees who would bring him food. Sadly, his story is one with a violent end.

One evening in 2001, 22-year-old Yuliana Romanova was passing through the crowded Mendeleyevskaya station with her pet Staffordshire bull terrier. They came across Malchik in a pedestrian underpass. Here stories differ, some say Malchik barked at the pair, others that he was laid down sleeping when they approached. At any rate, instead of walking on by, Romanova reached into her rucksack, drew out a kitchen knife, and to the shock of the many commuters nearby, stabbed the stray dog no less than six times, killing him.

The story received widespread coverage in Russian media and Romanova was arrested and made to undergo a year of psychiatric treatment. Malchik's statue, which was funded by donations, commemorates his death, but also symbolises the struggles of the many strays that roam the capital, estimated to be around 35,000 in number.[14]

During 2009, around 500 of these stray dogs were believed to live in the stations, which are obviously warmer and drier than the outside. However, around twenty of these dogs developed an interesting behaviour that has intrigued animal behaviourists, for not only did they manage to descend the metro's vertiginous escalators, they also learned to ride the trains and seemingly to know where they were going!

There are three main ideas put forward to explain this remarkable ability. Firstly, the dogs were judging the length of time between stations. Secondly, they may have recognised the announcer's voices at the different stations and perhaps the names of the stations themselves. And thirdly, they may have become familiar with the different smells at the different stations. Perhaps most likely is that they used a combination of all three, along with other cues such as station lighting and recognising people who regularly embark and disembark at certain stops.[15]

Another skill the dogs possessed was that of knowing which humans were likely to be friendly and which less so. They consistently only approached those who were sympathetic to them.

What the dogs revealed is how adaptable they can be. Metros are the sort of busy, noisy places that many dogs would find confusing and stressful, but these animals, perhaps because of the rewards of food, warmth, human companionship, and a regular routine, learned to overcome such fears and were often found sleeping in the centre of busy concourses and packed train compartments.

Of course, not all the stray dogs were friendly. In 2007, there were 20,000 dog attacks in the area, some of which have been traced to status dogs that have been abandoned by their owners. Dogs can also be a nuisance in other less serious ways, for example by carrying out the so-called bark-and-grab – a technique where a dog will suddenly bark loudly behind a person eating, causing them to drop their food. (I hope my dog doesn't read this and get ideas).

As a result, since around 2013 metro employees have been tasked with trying to keep the dogs out of the stations and if you are in Moscow it is rare now to see a subway-riding dog. You will, however, certainly be able to see Malchik's beautiful statue.

For more rail-travelling dogs, see Chapter 7.

Giro – Nazi dog?

Back in the UK, at the foot of a large tree, behind some railings and encased, rather oddly, in a Plexiglas container can be found the gravestone of little Giro. It's a bit wonky, but the German inscription is still clearly visible and translates thus:

> 'Giro'
> A faithful companion!
> London February 1934
> Hoesch

The memorial sits beside 9 Carlton House Terrace, which is now home to The Royal Society, but was once the German Embassy. How, you may ask, did a so-called Nazi dog get to be buried just a stone's throw from Buckingham Palace and the Palace of Westminster?

To find the answer we must turn our attention to the dog's owner, Leopold von Hoesch. Hoesch was the German ambassador to Britain from 1932 until his untimely death in 1936. It was his task to maintain good Anglo-German relations and this he did very well, being a natural diplomat who was much liked by the British Foreign Secretaries of the time. When Hoesch first came to Britain he represented the liberal and progressive Weimar Republic, but in 1933 everything changed with Hitler's rise to power. By default, Hoesch now represented the National Socialist German Workers' Party.

FIGURE 113: Pack of dogs checking out the Leningradsky rail station.

Hoesch's views were at odds with much of the Nazi's ideology and he seems to have been a brave and outspoken critic of the new regime. He was particularly worried by the extreme views of some in the party, such as the arrogant and vain Joachim von Ribbentrop. Hoesch sent repeated communications to Hitler about his misgivings and was probably a source of some exasperation to the Führer. Sadly, in 1936, Hoesch died aged just fifty-five, from a heart attack while at the embassy. Some reports suggest that desperately trying to maintain good relations with Britain in such politically uncertain times may have contributed to his death.[16]

Hoesch was given a funeral procession with full military honours attended by a number of British dignitaries. Archive footage of the event shows his coffin draped in a large Nazi flag as it travels down the Mall on its way towards Victoria station – a sobering thought considering what was to come. Hoesch's final journey back home to Germany was on board the British destroyer *HMS Scout*. He was buried in Dresden, but it is said that not one member of the Nazi party paid their respects at his funeral.

And what of his dog, Giro? Hoesch brought his canine companion (sometimes referred to as a small terrier and at other times as a German shepherd) with him when he first came to London. However, poor Giro did not last long. Just two years after arriving at the embassy, he died from electrocution while chewing through some cables.[17] His tombstone was initially in the garden of 9 Carlton House Terrace, but during some renovations to the house in the 1960s it was moved and placed by the tree, where it stands today. Giro's remains are presumably still in their original spot in the garden.

After his death, Hoesch was replaced by the very man he most distrusted, Von Ribbentrop, who immediately set about giving the embassy a Nazi makeover. It is said that there is still a swastika mosaic on one of the floors, beneath a carpet. Von Ribbentrop wasn't in residence long, however, before the outbreak of war saw him go back to Germany. Hoesch was clearly a good judge of character, as Ribbentrop apparently abandoned his own dog, a chow chow – something that didn't go down well with the *Daily Mirror* who reported how it typified Nazism.[18] In fact, Ribbentrop would go on to play a brutal part in the events that followed and was hung for war crimes a year after the war ended.

In his blog, *Darkest London*, Marc Haynes eloquently states, 'the little tombstone's not simply a marker of where a dog is buried, but something much bigger. It's a memorial not just to a dog that was loved by its master, but to von Hoesch himself – and a testament to how love ultimately endures as hate withers.'[19]

FIGURE 114: 'GIRO', a true companion!

FIGURE 115: Just Nuisance will be forever remembered in Simon's Town, South Africa.

JUST A NUISANCE

If you have a cat or dog you may have noticed that they sometimes like to lie in the most inopportune places. Halfway down a steep, poorly lit stairway for example, or, in the case of my dog at the intersection between the hall and the kitchen. I suspect that she chooses this area, as it enables her to easily and effectively intercept any evening raid we may wish to make on the fridge or biscuit tin.

One dog who owed his name to such behaviour was the Great Dane, Just Nuisance, but in this case he would sprawl on the busy decks of ships and frequently at the top of the gangplank. Bearing in mind his breed and the fact that he stood 6ft 6in on his hind legs, it's not surprising that he tended to get in the way a lot – hence his name.

Just Nuisance was born in 1937 and lived with his owner, Benjamin Chaney, in Simon's Town, a Royal naval base in South Africa. Being an outgoing sort of dog, he soon made friends with the sailors who treated him to such doggy delights as pies and cakes. Not surprisingly, Just Nuisance liked to follow the generous sailors wherever they went, including into the local bars (where he would down a pint of beer in record time) and even on trains to Cape Town, such as when the sailors went on leave.[20]

These last excursions got our canine commuter into trouble, as he rarely had a ticket and the conductors soon became fed up with his fare-dodging ways. At first they put him off the train at the next station, but somehow he always managed to board another

service. In the end, the rail company got so fed up that they began demanding Just Nuisance's owner, Chaney, either keep his dog away from the station, pay for his tickets, or have him put down.

The local Royal Navy sailors were so upset at the thought of the dog being put to sleep that they petitioned on his behalf to the Naval Commander in Chief, who had an excellent idea – Just Nuisance would be enlisted into the Royal Navy, so that way he would officially be their mascot and, more to the point, would be eligible for free rail travel.

Just Nuisance was soon to rise in the ranks. Despite some less than perfect behaviour, such as repeatedly losing his collar and sleeping on an officer's bed, he was quickly promoted to Able Seaman. This meant he got free rations as well as travel! Interestingly, Just Nuisance is thought to be the only signed-up sailor never to have set sail. However, he still did his bit for the Navy on land: attending parades at which he wore a rakish sailor's cap, raising funds, and most definitely boosting morale.

BAMSE: A LINK BETWEEN NATIONS

Unlike Just Nuisance, Bamse the St Bernard did travel the oceans. He was taken to sea as a mere pup, although this apparently didn't prevent him getting seasick. Bamse (meaning 'bear' in Norwegian) was the pet of Erling Hafto, a Norwegian naval lieutenant on the patrol boat *Thorodd*. This huge dog soon showed himself to be fiercely patriotic. It is said that he would stand by the gun tower wearing his specially made steel helmet and bark angrily at enemy planes.[21]

In June 1940, the *Thorodd*, including Bamse, made her escape from Nazi-occupied Norway to Scotland. Here she was converted for use as a minesweeper before being stationed throughout the rest of the war in Dundee and Montrose.

Like Just Nuisance, Bamse seems to have been fond of public transport. So that he could travel on the local buses, the sailors got him a bus pass that he wore in a plastic wallet round his neck. It is said that he would disembark at various stops and round up the sailors to take them back to port.[21]

Bamse was not a fan of violence, for when any of the crewmates got into a fight he would intervene, skilfully manoeuvring his large body between the warring factions and occasionally jumping up and placing his massive paws on their shoulders. He is also credited with rescuing a drunken sailor who had fallen into the water and preventing a Norwegian officer from being mugged.[21]

With all these accolades it's not surprising that Bamse soon became not just a mascot of the Royal Norwegian Navy, but of all the Free Norwegian Forces. A photograph of him sporting a Royal Norwegian Navy cap was added to Christmas and Easter cards sent throughout the war and he became a symbol of Norwegian resistance.

After Bamse died from heart failure in 1944, he was buried with military honours at Montrose, where many gathered to watch his funeral procession including Norwegian and British servicemen and 800 school children. But his story didn't end there. Every ten years the Royal Norwegian Army has held a commemorative ceremony for him.

In 2006, with the publication of a popular book, the story of Bamse reached a whole new generation.[22] His grave was restored and a larger-than-life monument was unveiled by the Duke of York in Montrose.

In 2009, a duplicate statue was transported from Scotland to Honningsvåg in Norway. The bond Bamse helped to foster between the nations is touchingly shown by the fact that the Bamse in Montrose looks northeast to Norway, while his double in Honningsvåg faces southwest to Montrose.

Pee and Poo!
Het Zinneke

What is it with Brussels and pee? First there was the little peeing boy, Manneken Pis, who was installed back in 1619 and went on to inspire a million little-boy-peeing fountains in gardens all over the world. In 1987, he was joined by a little peeing girl, Jeanneke Pis. And finally, in 1998, local sculptor Tom Frantzen created a canine version. This little bronze dog, which is modelled on Frantzen's own pet, is positioned cocking his leg up against a Brussels street bollard.

The Shit Fountain

In Chicago, the artist Jerzy S. Kenar has installed a fountain at the edge of his garden as a not-so-subtle reminder to those walking their dogs not to allow them to defecate and trample on his flowers. Set on a stone plinth it features, yep, a large bronze poo. What we really need of course is dogs who clean up after themselves. Happily for the people of Yekaterinburg in Russia, there is one who does just that!

FIGURE 116 (opposite): Our Scottish Bamse looks north-east to his counterpart in Norway.

FIGURE 117: One of three peeing statues in Brussels.

FIGURE 118 (right): The sort of dog we'd all like to own (Yekaterinburg, Russia).

REFERENCES

1. Cats in York website, http://catsinyork.com.
2. https://www.thecatgallery.co.uk/The-York-Cat-Trail.
3. French, R., *The Cats of Kuching, Malaysia*, The Saturday Paper, 15 April 2017.
4. Wikipedia, https://en.wikipedia.org/wiki/Kuching.
5. Wikipedia, https://en.wikipedia.org/wiki/Kuching_Cat_Museum.
6. Modis, C., *History Matters: Operation Cat Drop*, Newsletter of the Association of former WHO staff, April 2005.
7. Thomas, J., Bosco, *Sunol's Dog Mayor, Lives on in Spirit*, The Mercury News, 22 August 2013.
8. 'Bosco the Dog Mayor' Bronze Portrait Statue – http://lenatoritch.com/project/bosco-the-dogmayor.
9. *A Shaggy Dog Story*, https://reverendhellfire.wordpress.com/2013/05/26/a-shaggy-dog-story.
10. http://lenatoritch.com.
11. Quasha, J., *Is Your Cat Two-Timing You?*, Fox News opinion, 20 July 2011.
12. Mandybur, J., *Jerk Cat Tricks Two Owners into Giving Him Double the Love*, Mashable.
13. Kean, H., *Traces and Representations: Animal Pasts in London's Present,* The London Journal, 36(1), p.54.
14. Sternthal, S., *Moscow's Stray Dogs*, The Financial Times, 16 January 2010.
15. Boyd, J., *How Did Moscow's Stray Dogs Learn to Navigate the Metro?*, Conversation, 18 February 2016.
16. *Von Hoesch Dies: German Diplomat; Ambassador to London, Under Strain since Locarno Coup, Succumbs to Heart Attack*, New York Times, 11 April 1936.
17. Velten, H., 2013, *Beastly London: A History of Animals in the City*, Reaktion Books, UK.
18. Kean., H., 2017, *The Great Cat and Dog Massacre: The Real Story of World War Two's Unknown Tragedy*, University of Chicago Press.
19. Haynes, M., Darkest London, https://darkestlondon.com/2011/11/10/giro-londons-favourite-dead-nazi-dog.
20. Simonstown.com, http://www.simonstown.com/just-nuisance.
21. Bondeson, J., 2011, *Amazing Dogs: A Cabinet of Canine Curiosities*, Cornell University Press, New York.
22. Whitsun, A., and A. Orr, 2009, *Sea Dog Bamse: World War II Canine Hero*, Birlinn Ltd, Edinburgh.

Conclusions

I hope you have enjoyed reading the stories behind the statues and are encouraged to go and see some of them yourself. If you have a picture or a story of your visit, please do let me know via the Monumental Tales website. I'd love to hear from you. It would also be great to be informed about any other memorials or monuments to pets you may come across, wherever they might be in the world.

Having read a lot about these statues, I can reveal that it was quite a magical moment when I finally encountered them in real life. I remember walking through Battersea Park on a beautiful day in early August. I had never been to the park before and was impressed with its size, lakes, and gardens. I almost felt like I was in another country, discovering a new place even though it is just a thirty-minute train ride from home. As I turned the corner in a shady, woodland path, there before me was the little brown dog statue. I feel embarrassed to admit it, but knowing the statue's back story, I felt a few tears prick my eyes. What a lucky thing no one else was there to see this sentimental, middle-aged woman sniffling. Someone had been there though, and recently, as fresh flowers were placed around the dog's front paws.

In Zelenogradsk, Russia, there is an unusual interactive statue of a cat looking out of a pretend window. You can sit beside this dapper, bowtie-wearing moggie and spin around with him as if on a carousel. The statue is dedicated to the many cats that live in the area who are, according to the local Cat Museum staff, 'very fine and fat!'

A Trip Advisor reviewer sums up wonderfully her feelings on discovering this unexpected piece of street art:

Figure 119: Monument to Zelenograd cats.

'Once in the small square with this sculpture, you feel so cheerful and weightless. What an interesting idea! . . . About this monument – childhood, holidays, cats. . . . Bravo masters who created such magnificence!'
AleSsia V, Georgievsk, Russia

I hope you find some similarly wonderful cat or dog statues on your travels.

All photographs Jackie Buckle except the following:
Fig. 1: Diana - Solomiya Trylovska/Shutterstock. *Fig. 2*: Seaman - Liz and Mary Clare https://www.flickr.com/photos/landmclare. *Fig. 3*: Chris Packham - David Foster Management. *Fig. 4*: Old Shep - Larry Kilmer https://www.flickr.com/people/84043478@N03/.
CHAPTER 1: *Fig. 7*: African wildcat - Sonelle Wikipedia https://en.wikipedia.org/wiki/GNU_Free_Documentation_License. Fig. 8: Bastet - Rama GNU Free Documentation License. *Fig. 9*: Anubis statue - Jon Bodsworth, Egypt Archive. Wikimedia Creative Commons Attribution-Share Alike 3.0. *Fig. 10*: Diana - Solomiya Trylovska/Shutterstock. *Fig. 12*: Maneki Neko - Yuta Sakaguchi. *Fig. 13*: St Roch - BasPhoto / Shutterstock. *Fig. 14*: Dog gargoyle -Ian Hainsworth / Alamy Stock Photo. *Fig. 15*: Cat in St Bartholomew's Church - Jan Armitage /https://www.facebook.com/allcatsarebeautiful/. *Fig. 16*: Wolsey - Ian Press/ Flickr - https://www. flickr.com/photos/ianpressphotography. *Fig. 19*: Tombili cat and statue - Anadolu Kedisi, Anatolian Cat https://anatoliancats.blogspot.co.uk.
CHAPTER 2: *Figs. 23-4*: Le Cimetere des Chiens et Autres Animaux Domestiques - Jean Pierre Collin, Nature Animale - http://www.natureanimale. com/. *Fig. 25*: Tiddles - Alison Hobson, Fairford History Soc archive. *Fig. 29*: Perce Blackborow on board ship with Mrs Chippy - Scott Polar Research Institute, University of Cambridge. *Fig. 30*: Mrs Chippy - Michael Gabriel. *Fig. 31*: Hachiko statue – M-Thanahum/Shutterstock. *Fig. 32*: Hachiko with Dr Hidesaburo - cowardlion/ Shutterstock. *Figs. 33-4*: Ruswarp statue – Joel Walker.
CHAPTER 3: *Fig. 36*: Churchill leaving Downing Street - Keystone Press/Alamy Stock Photo. *Fig. 38*: Larry - Charlotte Bransgrove. *Fig. 39*: Roosevelt Memorial - Carolyn M Carpenter/Shutterstock. *Fig. 40*: Lincoln - Travis Souther, MLIS. *Fig. 45*: Queen Victoria's dog – Sasimoto/ Shutterstock.
CHAPTER 4: *Fig. 47*: Boatswain - Nottingham City Museum. *Fig. 52*: Tennyson - Nick Stubbs/Shutterstock. *Fig. 53*: Robert Louis Stephenson - Richard Brunton, Flickr - https://www.flickr.com/photos/filmstalker/. *Fig. 54*: Robbie Burns – Steve Lovegrove/ Shutterstock.
CHAPTER 5: *Fig. 55*: Sallie - Randy G. Lubischer, Monmouth County, New Jersey, USA. *Fig. 56*: Cat on propeller - © Imperial War Museums ( ) Q 73724. *Fig. 57*: Messenger dog - © Imperial War Museums ( ) Q9276. *Fig. 58-9*: Ilford Pet cemetery – Helen Cobb. *Fig. 61*: Smoky - Franck Fotos/Alamy Stock Photo. *Fig. 62*: Guam statue – Wikimedia https://creativecommons.org/publicdomain/mark/1.0/deed.en. *Fig 63*: National K9 memorial - Carrie-Ann McNabb and @polscotdogs. *Fig. 64*: Bretagne - Lena Toritch http://

LenaToritch.com. *Fig. 65*: Arson K-9 National Fire Dog Monument - State Farm, Flickr - https://www.flickr.com/photos/statefarm. *Fig. 66*: Bunkou © Blanscape | Dreamstime.com
CHAPTER 6: *Fig. 67*: Puss in Boots – Carlin Joe, Flickr - https://www.flickr.com/photos/carlinjoe/. *Fig. 71*: Bremen Town Musicians - Bildagentur Zoonar GmbH/Shutterstock. *Fig. 72*: Latvia Town Musicians - Orskis/Shutterstock. *Fig. 72-3*: Beddgelert photos - © Copyright Ian King - photography.wales. *Fig. 77*: Legend of the cats - Coralie/Shutterstock. *Fig. 78*: Girl cat – Ginette Fisher - http://gigi66.canalblog.com/. *Fig. 79*: Wagyha - Puru Pawar - https://www.flickr.com/photos/purupawar/. *Fig. 80*: *A Dog of Flanders* – Fouquier Flickr. *Fig. 81*: Hairy Maclary – Paul Cuming - https://www.flickr.com/photos/birdo.
CHAPTER 7: *Fig. 83*: Pavlov - Catriona Bass Russian Images/Alamy Stock Photo. *Fig. 84*: Laboratory cat statue -Viola Bz - http://vsuete.com/about/. *Fig. 88*: Laika - DE ROCKER/Alamy Stock Photo. *Fig. 89*: Matthew Flinders Donington – Guy Erwood/Shutterstock. *Fig. 91*: Bobbie - Thomas Schrantz, Flickr. *Fig. 92*: Balto - Photo 59806080© Nylakatara2013 - Dreamstime.com. *Fig. 93*: Balto and Togo in snow - FitchDnld, Flickr, https://www.flickr.com/people/30706946@N00/. *Fig. 94*: Lampo - LepoRello (Wikipedia Commons). *Fig. 95*: Red Dog – Richard Giles, Flickr, https://www.flickr.com/photos/richardgiles/. *Fig. 96*: Towser statue and kittens - Fraser Band http://www.fraserband.co.uk/. *Fig. 97*: Jim the Wonder Dog - Robin Woltman. *Fig. 98*: McKensie Sheepdog - Ng Zheng Hui/Shutterstock. *Fig. 99*: Nipper - Andy Rankin, Flickr https://www.flickr.com/photos/rankinstones/.
CHAPTER 8: *Fig. 105*: Great cat Kuching - © Ravindran John Smith - Dreamstime.com. *Fig. 106*: Giant cat family - Mazur Travel/Shutterstock. *Fig. 107*: Cats of Kuching - Allan Lawrence, Flickr - https://www.flickr.com/photos/ grey_albatross/. *Fig. 108*: Bosco - Lena Toritch/Young Fine Art Studio - http://lenatoritch.com/. *Fig. 109*: Monty - Kgbo Wikipedia Creative Commons Attribution-Share Alike 4.0 International license. *Fig. 110*: Hamish McHamish - Michael Laing. *Fig. 111*: Statue to homeless cats - Wikimedia Dat doris [CC BY-SA 4.0]. *Fig. 112*: Malchik - Dave Odgers, Flickr https://www.flickr.com/photos/95033437@N00/. *Fig. 113*: Russian dog pack - Tim Adams, Flickr - https://www.flickr.com/ people/36217981@N02/. *Fig. 115*: Just Nuisance - Quality Master/Shutterstock. *Fig. 116*: Bamse - Kathryn White, Flickr - https://www.flickr.com/people/80190531@N06/. *Fig. 117*: Peeing dog - Santi Rodriguez / Shutterstock.com. *Fig. 118*: Monument to the 'cultural' dog - Sergei Afanasev/Shutterstock.
CONCLUSIONS: *Fig. 119*: Zelenograd cat - Irina Borsuchenko/Shutterstock.

FURTHER READING

In addition to the books referenced in the text I would also like to recommend the following:
Gardiner, J. 2006, *The Animals' War: Animals in Wartime from the First World War to the Present Day*, Portrait, London
Lambton, L., 2011, *Palaces for Pigs: Animal architecture and other beastly buildings*, Atlantic Monthly Pr., London
Lambton, L., 1986, *Beastly Buildings: The National Trust Book of Architecture for Animals*, Historic England Publishing, London
Lambton, L., 1992, *Lucinda Lambton's Magnificent Menagerie: Or, Queer Pets and Their Goings-On*, Harper Collins, London
MacDonogh, K., *Reigning Cats and Dogs: A History of Pets at Court Since the Renaissance*, St Martin's Press, London
Malek, J., 1993, *The Cat in Ancient Egypt*, The British Museum Press/The Natural History Museum, London
Pickens, J.B., 2012, *Pets at the White House: 50 Years of Presidents and their Pets* Fife and Drum Press, USA
Street, P. 2017, *Animals in the Second World War*, The History Press, Stroud
Tague, I.H., *Animal Companions: Pets and Social Change in Eighteenth-Century Britain*, Penn State University Press, Pennsylvannia,
Toms J., 2006. *Animal Graves and Memorials* (Shire Album). A comprehensive and beautifully illustrated guide.
Velten, H., 2013, *Beastly London: A History of Animals in the City*, Reaktion Books, UK
Vocelle, L.A., 2016, *Revered and Reviled: A Complete History of the Domestic Cat*, The Great Cat, USA
Walker-Meikle, K., 2014, *Medieval Pets*, The British Library Publishing Division, London

BV - #0022 - 100720 - C150 - 248/184/10 - PB - 9780718895457